HENRY MOORHOUSE

Henry
Moorhouse

John MacPherson

40 Beansburn, Kilmarnock, Scotland

ISBN-13: 978 1 909803 87 9

www.ritchiechristianmedia.co.uk

Typeset by John Ritchie Ltd., Kilmarnock
Printed by Bell & Bain Ltd., Glasgow

PREFACE TO THE POPULAR EDITION.

THE remarkable religious awakening which is generally known as "the Revival of 1859," arose, in a sort of spiritual succession to the American Revival of 1857–58, in Ulster; it had also a powerful effect upon the religious life of England and Scotland, and in that time of glorious harvest many were converted who subsequently became active in the work of God. So far as Great Britain is concerned, this was the chief Revival movement of the century, among the masses. It was not so widespread as to transform the condition of the whole country, as did the great Evangelical Revival of the previous century; but this desirable result was certainly attained in Ulster, where the days of '59 were the most wonderful, in a spiritual sense, that had ever been known.

Among the converts in England who immediately began to witness for God, was HENRY MOORHOUSE. At first, his voice was heard in humble gatherings of work-people; then he was out in the highways and byways, preaching and tract-distributing, and in all things endeavouring to win souls for his Master. Gradually, as he devoted himself to the study of the Oracles of Truth, it was seen, as he compared scripture with scripture and brought forth "things new and old" from the heavenly treasure-house of the Word, that he possessed a singular gift for Bible-teaching. The Book seemed to glow again as its mighty truths were depicted and described, and their beautiful harmony was shown. The simplicity of the preacher, and the ingenuousness of his manner, had emphatically a charm of their own ; but the real attraction of the preaching of Henry Moorhouse was peculiarly in the cross of Christ and the glory and power of redeeming love.

Moorhouse, in his use of the Bible, was "a man apart" in the sphere of evangelism. Like others of his day, he rose from the ranks of the poor, and broke from associations with drunkards and music-hall frequenters—and the "sing-song" of the mid-Victorian day was debased indeed. From such a quagmire of sin and folly he emerged, riveting the interest of great audiences, and creating not merely a strong affection for himself—which he counted as nothing—but a sense of joy and delight in Redemption's plan, and in the lovely pages of prophet and apostle, wherein, by the inspiration of the Spirit, that plan is set forth. In two continents the name of Moorhouse came to be sufficient, among many people, to arouse deep interest and profound attention.

Of education, he had little or none ; yet he was familiar with the ways of men, and developed a wonderful gift for winning the ear of the multitude. His personal appearance was by no means calculated to impress, so frail was he, so boyish in simplicity ; but when once his tongue was unloosed, and the stores of his warm heart and alert mind were brought forth, men were fascinated by his glowing words, being, moreover, the more surprised that so much

skill and so much fervour lay hidden beneath so ordinary
an exterior; wherefore, as he expounded Scripture,

> still the wonder grew
> That one small head could carry all he knew.

Indeed, people who knew him only by reputation could
scarcely conceal their amazement on learning that the
"great preacher," announced on some foolishly drawn-up
"mammoth poster" in American cities, could be the frank
youth, with an engaging smile and a huge Bible, whom
they met at the railway-station. Men have a way of ex-
pecting a distinguished preacher who is unknown to them,
to prove to be, if not necessarily of massive build and
dominating appearance, at any rate personally impressive.
For example, of that wonderful apostle of Revival, James
Turner, of Peterhead, a cold and unbelieving professor
of Christianity, growled, as the cough-twisted consumptive
ascended the pulpit : " Do you call *that* a Revivalist ? "
And when the naive and cherubic Moorhouse appeared
on a platform, turning the pages of his Bible with care
and precision, a ripple of surprise, if not of amusement,
was apt to sweep through the audience. Only for a
moment, however ; only for a moment. When the quaint
little man began, without a touch of self-consciousness, to
speak from the Word of God, light flashed forth from the
glorious pages.

To appreciate the position of Moorhouse in the Revival,
we need to understand that the movement itself was
somewhat, though not entirely, apart from the churches.
The Anglican clergy and the Nonconformist ministry were
perhaps, with notable exceptions like Baptist Noel, a little
puzzled at the idea of men like Reginald Radcliffe, the

lawyer ; Brownlow North, the former roué and sportsman :
Hay Macdowall Grant, the Highland laird; and Richard
Weaver, once a drunken, blaspheming coal-miner—being
allied in evangelism, and, with many another like-minded
preacher, scouring the whole country in campaigns of soul-
winning.   "Laymen" as they were, such men therefore
had about them, according to the judgment of those
days, a touch of the free-lance adventurer.   Was not the
ministry available ?   Were not the pulpits of Great Britain
and Ireland sufficient ?   Would not this irruption, into the
preaching sphere, of unordained men, bring religion into
contempt ?   And, while churches and chapels were half
filled, was it not unreasonable to conduct evangelistic
services, for the ragtag and bobtail of the community, in
town   halls   and   theatres   and   circuses ;   in   parks   and
market-places ?

Brownlow North, it is true, received the welcome of the
ministerial majority of the Free Church of Scotland, and
was officially appointed an evangelist ; Hay Aitken found a
place of high usefulness as a pioneer of evangelisation for
the Church of England ; but, speaking generally, the main
body of the preachers who were associated with that Revival
were men who had little regard for differences between
what is "clerical" and what is "lay," but who, going back
to the Bible as their warrant and commission, were content
to be regarded as the "offscouring of all things," if they
might by any means win souls for Christ.   Some of these
were associated with the Christians usually designated
Open Brethren ; but all were so entirely given up to
principles and methods that unite, that they scarcely gave
a thought to questions that sunder.   Of organisation

among themselves, the Revival preachers had none, and sought none. Radcliffe, being frequently looked to for counsel and guidance, would find many an opening for the evangelists, and was perhaps the best-known English layman of the movement ; but he was so self-effacing and was so given to Gospel efforts away from the beaten track of religious endeavour, that history has taken less notice of him than his career, so crowded with zealous and fruitful endeavour, seems to demand.

Among this company of "Revival men," then, stood Moorhouse. There were others more demonstrative than he in the rugged force which makes so deep an impression upon a mixed multitude ; but there was perhaps no man of his time who, by the grace of God, was so apt in wielding the Sword of God—the Word of Life.

The biography, by Rev. John Macpherson, was prepared soon after Moorhouse (at the early age of forty) passed to his rest. The material at command was sufficient if not ample, although Moorhouse always had the strongest objection to anything in the shape of press puffs, the "limelight" of this world possessing no attraction for him. During the years that have lapsed since the biography was issued, a few new facts have come to light ; and some which actually did receive Mr. Macpherson's recognition have been rendered of deeper interest through the publication of biographies of men of God who knew Moorhouse—notably that of Dwight Lyman Moody. It may be permitted, therefore, by way of preface to the "Popular" edition, to add a few further words regarding Moorhouse and his career as an evangelist and Bible expositor and teacher.

Perhaps those who knew him best were Richard Weaver

and John Hambleton.   The latter, rugged and uncon-
ventional—a man for the race-course and the fair and
the great audience of working-class people—often had
Moorhouse for his companion in preaching and Bible-
selling.   They had many an adventure together, and not
infrequently found themselves at cross purposes with the
world.   For instance, at the Shakespeare Tercentenary
celebration at Stratford-on-Avon, in 1864 (to which Mr.
Macpherson refers), Hambleton, Moorhouse, and Edward
Usher went out into the streets bearing boards inscribed
with "awakening" mottoes.   A splendid procession of
ecclesiastical and educational dignitaries passed along,
and the three evangelists counter-marched in single file.
Doubtless, the proceeding struck the great and learned men
who were doing honour to Shakespeare's memory as ill-
timed and fanatical; but the three were determined "not
to know anything among you, save Jesus Christ": they
would live to witness for the truth as it is in Jesus, and to
that alone; being, indeed, called thereto.   Moorhouse,
moving about amid the crowd near the pavilion where the
celebration meetings were held, was threatened with removal
as a "nuisance."   Presently a crowd came forth from a con-
cert, when the sight of the text-boards, once again, in the
midst of all the rejoicings in the "swan of Avon," was too
much for the British public; so the three found themselves
the centre of an angry mob, who tore up the evangelists'
tracts and flung the pieces in their faces.   Turning,
however, from the votaries of literature and music to the
humble peasantry, Moorhouse and his friends held meetings
in the neighbouring fields, when many seeking souls were
led to Christ.   Thus, while Shakesperean scholars were

rejoicing in the delicate beauty of " Hark! hark ! the lark at heaven's gate sings," or in the humanness of " Blow, blow, thou winter wind," these three simple-hearted men, with the old message that alone can transform and satisfy, were singing—while the cry of penitent souls seeking the Lord resounded among the trees—the glorious Revival song :

> My heart is fixed, Eternal God,
> Fixed on Thee ;
> And my immortal choice is made—
> Christ for me :
> He is my Prophet, Priest, and King,
> Who did for me salvation bring ;
> And while I've breath I mean to sing,
> Christ for me !

Another experience, to which Mr. Macpherson also makes passing reference, was at Epsom. Moorhouse and Hambleton were conducting meetings in a tent, at Dorking, and desired to witness for Christ in the midst of the Epsom saturnalia—not far away. It was the custom in that day to suggest that Epsom race-course is "no place for religion," and it was perhaps on this account that the Gospel was heard but little amid the enormous concourse of people assembled on the " Derby " day. It was known, too, that the sound of hymn-singing was particularly offensive on such a day to the wealthy people in the grand stand, and in the special "enclosures " which are the resort of monied men and women who desire to gamble. Open-air missioning, too, had largely fallen into desuetude in this country, despite the example, away back in the centuries, of Wickliffe's Poor Preachers, and despite the fact that the repressive legislation of the Stuarts had so long given place to a glorious freedom for the proclamation of Christ crucified—of which Whitefield and Wesley had taken full advantage in the eighteenth century. Whatever the "racing industry" or the Pall Mall club-men might think, Moorhouse and Hambleton were determined to speak fo the Lord, and declare the saving message of life eternal, whether the people would hear or whether they would forbear. The two evangelists each bore one of the familiar text-boards. One was inscribed: "Jesus Only," and the other: "God is Love." They had speedily to suffer for what the world called "eccentricity"; for it is a fact not without its humorous aspect that the children of this world, in arguing for the total exclusion of the Gospel from their scenes of riot, actually assume an air of holy horror, and affect to believe that it is solely in championship and defence of the Christian message that they would shut that message out!

From the vast crowd of race-goers—which included dirty tramps and swarms of thieves, as well as gorgeously attired ladies from Mayfair and many representatives of aristocratic and mercantile England—there was inevitably scant sympathy; for them, "Jesus Only" and "God is Love" created only a sense of boredom or of positive annoyance; nevertheless, the two preachers toiled on, witnessing and exhorting, despite the showers of orange-peel, fish-bone, and egg-shell, with which they were assailed.

Such experiences, however little in harmony with the views of the distinguished leaders of pleasure of this present world, made a splendid "apprenticeship" for Moorhouse. He was in early manhood, fresh from Manchester streets, without any bondage of preconceived ideas that would hold him to pursue the regular methods of orthodoxy. There was little or no opportunity for such a man if he trod the beaten path. Moreover, what college would accept a fragile youth who looked fitter to play cricket with little boys on a village green than to preach the mighty truths of the Gospel? Not that Moorhouse had any thought of seeking such opportunity. His governing principle in life was to do the will of God: hence, he followed where God led; and that guidance led him, not into the schools of men, but into the school of everyday "rough-and-tumble" life. This, of course, is not to scout learning or to belittle the training and educational equip-ment of the Christian ministry; but, after all, the progress of the Kingdom of God is of greater import than the maintenance of old scholastic methods. Moorhouse, raised up to preach the Gospel, and blessed with a conspicuous gift, could not remain silent.

The Churches have perhaps not been aware of the effects of what may be called the evangelistic side of the Brethren Movement. Moorhouse, moving in that circle, and giving himself to ardent study, became, as the years passed, emphatically a "Bible" evangelist and teacher; and it is no difficult matter to trace much of the revived interest in the Holy Scriptures (which, although seldom recog-nised, marked the later years of the nineteenth century and the beginning of the twentieth, and which still con-tinues) to the boyish preacher from Manchester. True, this return to the Bible began with the origin of Brethrenism. It was the very essence of the testimony of George Müller, Anthony Norris Groves, Benjamin Wills Newton, William Kelly, and many another; but it is not too much to say that the truths of the written Word shone with fresh lustre for great numbers, in a new generation, under the Spirit-touched expositions that came so spontaneously from the artless lips of Moorhouse.

Perhaps the most telling illustration of what he was is to be found in the biography of Moody. Mr. Macpherson makes allusion to the incident of the week of Moorhouse's preaching from John 3 : 16 ; but in "The Life of Dwight L. Moody," the beloved American preacher's eldest son, Mr. W. R. Moody, reproduces the whole story in his father's own words. Moody had heard of Moorhouse as "the boy preacher"—an objectionable title which, however execrable to zealous evangelists, seems to exercise an equal fascination upon the secular press and upon shallow sensation-mongers, whose only thoughts are to secure, the one a huge circulation and the other a large collection. The unfavourable impression created by this unhappy designation was not removed when the two met, for Moorhouse "did not look more than seventeen"; hence, Moody would by no means encourage any friendliness. Soon after returning to Chicago, Moody received various letters from Moorhouse, proposing "to visit you and preach." But Moody's replies were coldness itself—all he would say was : "If you happen to come West, call on me." Finally, Moorhouse wrote that he was shortly arriving in Chicago, "and would preach." Upon this, Moody told the officers of the church : "There is an Englishman coming here on Thursday who wants to preach ; I don't know whether he can or not." Such an introduction scarcely being calculated to arouse fiery enthusiasm, the brethren expressed the opinion that as there were signs among the congregation of renewed interest in spiritual things, it would not be wise for a stranger to preach. However, Moody was to be away from Chicago for a few days, and he finally decided that Moorhouse might be conceded a trial on the Thursday; and then should he do pretty well, he might be invited to take part on the Friday also. " If he speaks well both nights," Moody added, "you will know whether to announce him or me for the Sunday. I will be back on Saturday." It was Moorhouse who was fixed for the Sunday.

" How is the young Englishman coming along ? " asked Moody of his wife, on returning to Chicago.

Mrs. Moody intimated that the people " liked him very much," adding : " He has preached two sermons from John 3 : 16. I think you will like him, although he preaches a little differently from you."

We can almost see the twinkle in Moody's eyes, and the alert turn of the head, as he asks : " How is that ? "

" Well," Mrs. Moody cheerfully admits, " he tells the worst sinners that God loves them."

" Then," says Moody, with characteristic emphasis and quickness, " he is wrong." But Mrs. Moody expressed the opinion : " I think you will agree with him when you hear him, because he backs up everything from the Bible."

To describe what followed, there is no way but to give Moody's simple statement :—

" Sunday came, and as I went to the church I noticed that every one brought his Bible. The morning address was to Christians. I had never heard anything quite like it. He gave chapter and verse to prove every statement he made. When night came the church was packed. ' Now,

beloved friends,' said the preacher, 'if you will turn to the
third chapter of John and the sixteenth verse, you will find
my text.' He preached the most extraordinary sermon
from that text. He did not divide the text into 'secondly'
and 'thirdly' and 'fourthly'; he just took the whole verse,
and then went through the Bible from Genesis to Revelation to prove that in all ages God loved the world. God
had sent prophets and patriarchs and holy men to warn us,
and then He sent His Son, and, after they killed Him, He
sent the Holy Ghost. I never knew up to that time that
God loved us so much. This heart of mine began to thaw
out ; I could not keep back the tears. It was like news
from a far country—I just drank it in. So did the crowded
congregation. I tell you there is one thing that draws
above everything else in this world, and that is love."

On the Monday, when the text, once again, was John
3 : 16, the sermon, Moody thought, "was better than the
other one ; he struck a higher note than ever, and it was
sweet to my soul to hear it. I used to preach that God
was behind the sinner with a double-edged sword ready to
hew him down. I preach now that God is behind him
with love, and that he is running away from the God of
love."

For six nights Moorhouse preached on this one text.
"The seventh night came, and he went into the pulpit.
Every eye was upon him. He said : 'Beloved friends, I have
been hunting all day for a new text, but I cannot find anything so good as the old one ; so we will go back to the
third chapter of John and the sixteenth verse'; and he
preached the seventh sermon from those wonderful words :
'God so loved the world.' I remember the end of that

sermon. ' My friends,' he said, ' I have been trying to tell you how much God loves you, but I cannot do it with " this poor stammering tongue." If I could borrow Jacob's ladder and climb up into heaven and ask Gabriel, who stands in the presence of the Almighty, to tell me how much love the Father has for the world, all he could say would be : " God so loved the world, that He gave His only begotten Son, that whosoever believeth in Him should not perish, but have everlasting life." ' "

It is impossible to read the life of Moorhouse without being convinced that the Divine plan for him, at any rate, was to go forth to the masses as an evangelist. Moreover, it may well be that his career has a lesson for the University and the Training College, in that it teaches what great things God may accomplish, according to His blessed will, through a man whose gifts are kindled into brilliancy by the light which shines from the Book of books, and to whom is given the wisdom of which the prophet spake when he declared : " He that winneth souls is wise." Truly says Charles Grandison Finney, in " Lectures on Revivals of Religion " : " A minister may be very learned and yet not *wise*. There are many ministers possessed of great learning ; they understand all the sciences—physical, moral, and theological ; they may know the dead languages and possess all learning, and yet not be wise in relation to the great end about which they are chiefly employed. An un-successful minister may be pious as well as learned, and yet not be wise. Those are the best-educated ministers who win the most souls. Learning is important, and always useful. But, after all, a minister may learn how to win souls to Christ without great learning, and *he* has the best education for a minister who can win the most souls for Christ."

During the three years prior to his death Moorhouse suffered much, but one of his chief desires was to encourage the sorrowing relatives and friends who ministered to him. To his little son he left, as a sort of spiritual legacy, the simple word—so full of wonderful meaning to one who preached so often upon "God so loved the world"—"God is Love." From the day when first he found Christ, until he was smitten down by his last illness, he had been incessant in his Master's service, and in that illness he glorified his Lord. Writing, only a few days before he died, to Major Whittle (to whom, in America, he had been the means of spiritual blessing), he said : "Dear loved brother,—Just out of bed ; first time for many a day. If I am not with the Lord, shall be real glad to see you next Tuesday ; but I am very ill. Ask prayer for me to suffer for Christ better than ever I preached for Him. I only want to glorify Him."

Gruff John Hambleton wrote thus tenderly of him just after the end came :—

" Our dear little brother has gone Home ; his great heart was too big for his frail little body. I stayed at his house three or four nights a week while labouring in Manchester during December [1880]. His sufferings were great ; he coughed for hours together ; but his happy smile throughout completely answered to that precious peace of soul reigning within. ' Oh, all right,' he would say, ' it is only a cough ; it would be worse if there were no cough.' Calling to see him just before he left us, I grasped his arms, as his face betokened that the enemy death was doing his last work, and said : ' Harry, we shall meet up yonder.' He replied, while gasping for breath : ' Sure, sure, sure ! '

" There was a native simplicity in this dear lad ever since he was brought to the Lord. We travelled together when he was about nineteen, and his little anecdotes would in two or three minutes bring a whole congregation into tears of joy. In his sleep, at that time, he would talk of Jesus, and often be as though he were preaching, saying of Christians : ' We ought to be more honest, more truthful ; living near to God. God wants *men* ; Christ wants *men* ; the Holy Ghost wants *men*—men of truth, men of God ! ' His growth in the knowledge of his Bible, in the years that followed, has been proved by his works, which will follow him. How plainly visible is the work of God in putting into such a little, frail vessel as our brother such a treasure, showing us all that the excellency of the power is of God, and not of us."

In a very real sense Moorhouse *learned* from the Bible. He was no lazy fellow, glad to cover his own carelessness by contempt for the acquirements of the laborious scholar. On the contrary, his devotion must have been most assiduous, or he could not have acquired so remarkable a mastery of the Scriptures. His tools seem to have been, as his "outlines" suggest, an ordinary Concordance, with perhaps a volume of " helps," and an occasional theological work ; he was endowed, too, with a splendid memory. Not only did he love the Word, but, in a way, he was " shut in " to it by the circumstances of his career ; and it must always be remembered that in the circle of the Brethren, wherein more particularly he moved, practically all were men of the one Book ; whereby he was doubtless encouraged and inspired in that "inside track" of Bible study as the exponent of which he came to excel.

Thus we see how a boisterous and unruly Lancashire lad—having only such rudiments of education as a factory-boy could acquire in days when the poor, as a class, were largely excluded, by their condition and by the lack of a State education system, from the possession of knowledge —at any rate endeavoured to teach himself somewhat ; and, "narrowing" his education down to the Book which is the revelation of Divine wisdom and Divine love, was taught of the Spirit. So, going forth to use his gift in the work of the Lord, he turned many to righteousness, and thus, as we may surely think, came within the ranks of the glorious company of whom that Book declares : "They that be wise shall shine as the brightness of the firmament ; and they that turn many to righteousness as the stars for ever and ever."

W. H. Harding.

AUTHOR'S PREFACE.

ONLY in the last years of his life did I know Henry Moorhouse. It is from this stand-point, necessarily, that I have written the following pages. The materials, apart from my own recollections and impressions, were not very abundant; his letters, especially, were few. Throughout his public career he cherished a strong repugnance to writing accounts of his work, fearing lest the rehearsal should lead to self-inflation and the dishonour of God. If in this he erred, he erred on the safe side. He had seen egotism on his high pinnacle, he had heard him blowing his foolish trumpet, he had witnessed his swift descent into unfathomable mire, and was greatly afraid. This fear kept him in the place of safety and usefulness ; and it imparted to his life and work a tone and quality of high excellence.

While many are loudly proclaiming that Christianity is effete, the ancient gospel that converted the persecuting Saul of Tarsus into a preacher of the faith he once laboured to destroy, changed the dissolute Corinthians into saints, and triumphed even in the palace of Nero, is still proving itself to be the power of God unto salvation. Although argument is to be met with argument, and the religion of Jesus is able to hold its own on the ground of truth and reason, the gainsayer is often most effectively met by the production of veritable specimens of the work the gospel proposes to accomplish. Such a specimen is furnished in the character and life of Henry Moorhouse. So long as the religion of Christ performs moral miracles of this kind, the assaults of unbelief will be in vain.

Further, when the gospel in its sublime excellence, its true divinity, its saving power, is pourtrayed on the broad canvas of a life full of beneficent labours, the picture possesses a rare interest for believing men and earnest workers, and may, by the blessing of God, stimulate them in the pursuit of holiness and in the promotion of the Christian cause. In a word, if the Holy Spirit should condescend to use this little book as the vehicle of His omnipotent grace, whether for the comfort of some or the conversion of others, it will surely be a matter of unspeakable gratitude and joy.

CONTENTS.

CHAPTER I.

EARLY DAYS 1   PAGE

CHAPTER II.

CONVERSION.. 9

CHAPTER III.

NEW LIFE 21

CHAPTER IV.

WORK IN ENGLAND AND WALES 35

CHAPTER V.

WORK IN AMERICA 47

CHAPTER VI.

THE WORLD FOR A PARISH 67

CHAPTER VII.

BIBLE TEACHING 87

CHAPTER VIII.

BIBLE SPREADING 112

CHAPTER IX.

LAST DAYS 122

CHAPTER X.

CHARACTER 133

HENRY MOORHOUSE.

CHAPTER I.

Early Days.

"And took his journey into a far country."—LUKE XV. 13.

Is the life of Henry Moorhouse worth recording?

An obscure Lancashire lad, in personal appearance puny and fragile, in speech rude and provincial, gifted with no wonderful powers, possessed of no learning, escaping by a rare marvel from the bottomless quag into which he had early plunged, becomes a preacher and a teacher ; a preacher whose words awaken sympathetic responses in the bosoms of many thousands on both sides of the Atlantic, and a teacher, not of babes, but of teachers—wise and able men being not ashamed to take a lesson in the wisdom he had learned in no man's school. A spark of wild fire, lurid and portentous, rising in the wilderness, borne hither and thither in the night, and ready to be quenched in its native marsh, is caught up into the firmament and becomes a star of no mean magnitude, whose silvery rays descend in blessing on the path of many a benighted wanderer. Who shall say that a light so curious calls for no investigation, deserves no passing notice?

HENRY MOORHOUSE was born in Lyon Street, Ardwick, Manchester, on the 27th September, 1840. His parents belonged to the rank and file of England's great army of honest working people, who are, as they have been, the real backbone of the nation's strength and greatness.

His father, by religion a Methodist, is described by Henry as "a kindly, upright man;" a sort of character, happily, not rare in that religious denomination, to which vital godliness among the masses of England owes so much. With whatever eccentricities of system or peculiarities of teaching, it is the glory of Methodism to proclaim salvation through a personal, divine, omnipotent Redeemer, a Gospel of free grace to every creature. And although good old-fashioned Methodism is supposed to touch the things of God with a rude hand, it fails not to put the essential matter in a shape so homely and crisp that the popular mind can grasp it, and the most illiterate take it in. Certainly he were a poor—indeed an utterly unworthy —Methodist, who did not strive to write on the first page of his child's memory "the Name that is above every name." Little Harry Moorhouse would doubtless hear the story of Jesus ere yet ear or heart had become familiar with aught beside the sweet sounds and peaceful ongoings of a pure home-life. Nor would there be wanting answers to those questions which a child of lively fancy and quick apprehension, like Harry, would put to his father regarding this simplest but profoundest of creeds, "Christ and Him crucified." At any rate, the name of the holy child Jesus would be inscribed on the child's memory, the story of the cross would be treasured up in some recess of the soul for a future day and purpose only known to God.

The elder Moorhouse was a teacher in Bank Meddon Sunday School. If glorying in ancestry were lawful or expedient, the son of a worthy under-shepherd of the great Christian flock might reckon he had as good reason to boast of his pedigree as any man in England. But if there be in this circumstance, the mere accident of birth, small ground for boasting, there is room for gratitude to Him, who, in His providence, as in all His ways, is "wonderful in counsel and excellent in working." The Sabbath-school teacher would take his little chubby-faced boy to school, where, in his tender years, and ere yet his mind was much pre-occupied with other things, he could learn the alphabet of Scripture knowledge. These lessons would be enforced at home. In the house of the consistent teacher there will always be a pure, healthful atmosphere ; the altar of God will occupy a high place, the lamp of the Word will be kept burning, the Lord's-day will be observed, order will be maintained, and life generally will be sweetened by "the nurture and admonition of the Lord." Such influences as those, doubtless, left a certain mark on the susceptible heart of little, quick-witted Harry Moorhouse.

Now, apart altogether from the work of grace in the conversion and sanctification of men, it frequently happens that the little store of Scripture truth treasured up in childhood's memory is in after-years, by the transforming touch of the Holy Spirit, transmuted into the fine gold of heavenly wisdom, and the very lessons of infancy thus become, in measure, the strength and beauty of the Christian character. Early impressions of truth are sometimes the hidden link by which God, in the purposes of His grace, prevents sinners from passing beyond the region of possible salvation into the dark, unknown land of utter reprobation. They are as *eyes* in conscience into which the hooks of the Gospel fasten. At any rate, most Christians in looking back on early life and training, will find occasion to mark with adoring gratitude the mercy that anticipated all their future, and directed their first feeble steps.

How much Henry Moorhouse owed to the Sabbath school, and to the teacher who added to his humble office the untold influence of a father's love, it is impossible to determine ; but there is reason to believe that the lessons of childhood, dimmed and blurred, and all but blotted out during the period of his wayward youth, came out again in wonderful vividness before the fire of the Holy Spirit, and became illuminated characters in his early Christian experience.   Teacher, be of good cheer !   It is yours to lay the wood and coals in order, which on some future day a celestial spark may kindle into a glowing fire.   Your work may, for the present, resemble a heap of stones from the quarry, shot out upon an unpromising site ; but the Holy Spirit is able of these rude materials to build within the soul the temple of God, whose very foundations shall be garnished with every precious stone.   Uncongenial is the soil of many a young heart into which the seeds of truth are dropped ; but under the quickening breath of the Lord, full often the buried germ comes forth in beauty and ripens into golden grain.   A handful of corn scattered on the mountain-top is a thin sowing on a hapless field, just so much good grain given to the frosts or to the fowls ; but one day a glorious sun arises on those arid peaks, and the seeds grow up like cedars, and a harvest waves with the glory of Lebanon.

At the age of twelve, Henry was put into employment in a shipping house, where, unhappily, he fell under the influence of wicked companions.   Work gave place to idle fooling and reckless pranks.   For his daring conduct in swinging on a " teagle " from a top story, he was by the master's advice removed by his father to a new sphere of occupation, in a spindle and fly works. This change wrought no improvement ; he loved the company of idle and foolish lads, and with them he would go.

The adventure of the " teagle " swing reveals not a little of his natural disposition, and partly explains the wild career on which he had now entered. He would outdo others in feats of daring, even if in so doing he should disregard all law and duty. To his ill-regulated fancy and foolish ambition, the very charm of heroism lay in madly passing beyond the limits of legitimate restraint and safety. And so he goes on to fresh adventures, to new forms of teagle-swinging from top-stories, finding greater zest, it may have been, in the perilous character of his ways than in the pleasures afforded by a life of sin.

About this time a new influence, at once gentle and powerful, began to operate as a partial check on his way-wardness. One who in subsequent years became more to him than all else in the world, was wont to meet him at school, and tried to win him for Christ. It was probably owing mainly to the influence of his faithful and gentle friend, Mary, that he continued to attend the Sabbath school; for, self-willed, impatient of all restraint, and mad upon his idols though he now was, his susceptible nature was unable wholly and at once to shake off the loving hand that sought to arrest him. Glorious and beyond all human comprehension is the sovereignty of God in the salvation of men ; yet, for the most part, the invisible hand of grace employs some tiny link in nature to keep the sinner from passing into the outer darkness, judicial blind-ness, and finally-sealed impenitence ; or, it may be, also to pave the way for the outgoings of mercy and the wanderer's return. It may be a mother's prayers, or a father's counsels, or a true-hearted woman's love, or a bitter memory, or an awe-inspiring dream, or the ineffaceable recollection of former happy days; but surely thus frequently does the Almighty Worker make use of some little thing to serve His highest ends, and so illustrate the glory of His own wisdom, power, and grace.

Although Mary did not succeed in winning him for Christ, her earnestness, her watchfulness, her love, held him in check for a time, and doubtless made a deep impression on his heart, despite the storms of sin that were now raging in his soul, and the dark clouds beginning to settle down upon his path.

"Ah, Harry! Harry!" from the bursting heart of his well-tried friend, was more powerful in his ears than any sermon could have been, in those days; but it was not sufficient to turn him from his ways. The work that needed to be wrought on him could not be effected by might or by power, but by the Spirit of the Lord. Despite counsels, expostulations, remonstrances, and tears, Henry pursued his wayward course, going from one depth of folly to a deeper still, till at length it seemed as if he would finally disappear in the shades of eternal night. "The wicked are like the troubled sea, when it cannot rest." Henry Moorhouse was no exception; his life was now a raving fever, a raging storm. He left his occupation and enlisted. It was a desperate attempt to quiet his conscience and keep his sin. In the army, as out of it, he was still the devoted soldier of Satan. His father, at serious cost, bought him off; but this kindness was cast to the winds: Henry went on in his dark career, going from bad to worse.

We must not draw aside the veil to gratify mere curiosity. Details of folly are little for edification. But we may not wholly conceal what Providence has not kept secret, lest we thereby diminish the Saviour's glory in so wonderful a trophy of His grace. Finally breaking through every restraint, neither filial love nor the endearments of home, neither the claims of honourable friendship nor the influences of the most tender affection, neither the self-respect common to men, nor the dread of consequences here or hereafter, held him any longer in check. Joining heart and soul in the companionship of the lawless and the profane, he became the sworn associate of men who feared neither God nor man.

Force of character there must have been, where a mere boy of sixteen could command rough, bearded men, far stronger and wilder than himself. Beside drink and other vices, he plunged into gambling. A prince among card players, he won money by handfuls. A "chief centre" in the principal gambling hell in Manchester, he was backed against all players by the Satan of the establishment, who pronounced Henry Moorhouse *facile princeps* on this diabolonian field. His adventures were sometimes desperate, but he was for the most part successful.

Possessing plenty of money, he spent it freely. Lost to all shame, one good thing remained in him. Even at his worst, he retained and cherished a feeling of pity for the poor. While a shilling was left him he could not pass a beggar without bestowing an alms. It was only nature; but it showed he was not past feeling, and the generous habit may have served to keep the spring of his affections from freezing into that icy solidity of selfishness which knows no thaw of penitence. So, men of wild passions and prodigal folly, who cherish some generosity of soul, sometimes find their way into the kingdom of God, when the mean, sordid, hollow-hearted professor of religion is left to pursue his course of respectable hypocrisy down to hell.

Amidst the high inflation of his animal spirits, the super-abounding merriment of jolly companionships, and the hey-day of successful sinning, Henry was often ill at ease. There was a skeleton in the cupboard, and the cupboard would now and again swing open. To face this grim thing he must needs carry on his person a loaded pistol, wherewith to shoot, not his neighbour, but himself, at what time the moment of despair might arrive. When he had spent his all, he would thus end all. In this there may have been an element of boyish bravado; but it shows he had reached that more remote region in the " far country," whence few return.

Every fresh step he took in the way of transgression became harder and harder. His lawless courses brought him into frequent collision with public order and justice; he was not unacquainted with a prison cell. Once and again, in fits of sheer wretchedness, he sought by various means to take his own life; but each time an unseen hand foiled the desperate attempt. Thus the sinner pursued his sin, and mercy pursued the sinner.

CHAPTER II.

𝔆𝔬𝔫𝔳𝔢𝔯𝔰𝔦𝔬𝔫.

"And he arose, and came to his Father."—LUKE XV. 20.

THE period in which the conversion of Henry Moorhouse took place was remarkable in the history of the Church of Christ. From 1857 to 1861, the Holy Spirit was poured out on whole churches and nations. Tidings of the great American revival were borne to this country like the breath of spring. It seemed to be the sounding of some mighty angel's trumpet summoning men to prayer. Here, there, everywhere, men assembled for the sole purpose of calling upon God. Answers to prayer, many and marked, suddenly became a striking feature of the movement. In church, in school, in cottage meeting, on green lawns, in highland glens, on lonely moors, in shops, in public-houses, in theatres, men were suddenly seized with a fear of God, a sense of eternal things, a belief in the efficacy of prayer, and a strong desire to obtain such mercies from heaven as may be dispensed at the throne of grace. In America, in Ireland, in England, in Scotland, and in many other parts of the world, the spirit of grace and supplication fell on the hearts of men of every creed and class, men without as well as within the Christian pale ; and, true to the letter of the Word, looking to the pierced One, mourning for sin and the joyful song of deliverance followed.

It was an epoch in the history of many hundreds of churches and many thousands of families and souls. Like the first great movement of the Holy Spirit in apostolic times, this work was not without its "signs and wonders." Marvellous answers to prayer, unexpected and astounding conversions, very miracles of grace, attested the special nearness and power of God. As, in illustration of His grace, the Master told the Jews that from the east and from the west, from the north and from the south, Gentile men should come and sit down with Abraham, and Isaac, and Jacob, in the kingdom of God, so now sinners from every quarter of the world and every point in the compass of human society were gathered into the living Church. From the highest regions of social life down to the lowest, the Lord Jesus called a new company of disciples. On the one hand, the almost unconquerable spirit of pride was cast down in the conversion of the high-born or the self-righteous; and, on the other hand, the foulest demons of vice were dispossessed the Saviour drew trophies from the slums. To that strange *terra incognita*, the more than African wilderness that is inhabited by the city Arab, the professional beggar, the pestilent loafer, the drunkard, the prostitute, the thief, and all the other poor, unknown, name-less things, mere fragments of humanity, shipwrecked in life, and cast hopeless on the cold shores of despair, the message of salvation was sent. As at the behest of an undeniable call, from those dark places many came forth, who, putting on Christ, began with bold testimony and new song to tell the world plainly that Jesus of Nazareth, the Friend of sinners, still lives. The world in its wisdom knew not what to make of this. It brought its measuring line, as is its wont; but this divine work was too high, too large, for the world's little tape. "Stop!" cried they, "we shall soon see the last of it." This means, "Wait a little; all those new Christians will either soon go back, or they will be dead and gone ; and then we shall have peace." But they did not go back ; and although many of them are no longer on earth, many a true story of holy life and self-sacrificing toil remains to attest the reality and power of grace. Of these, not the least remarkable, as a trophy of the Redeemer's power and a standard-bearer of the cross, was Henry Moorhouse.

In 1859–60, the work of God was making progress in various cities and towns of Lancashire. Labourers whom the Lord of the harvest had thrust into the field were reaping in plenty. The time was full of energy, hope, and joy. Great meetings were held in Manchester, where thousands, assembled in the Circus, in the Alhambra, and other places of meeting, were addressed by such well-known men as Wilbraham Taylor, Robert Baxter, Stevenson Blackwood, W. P. Lockhart, Reginald Radcliffe, Richard Weaver, Alfred Trench, Lord Radstock, and many more.

Among others converted at this period was Thomas Castle, one of Henry's companions in evil. The young convert lost no time in seeking out his friend, and in setting before him all the inducements to repentance which his own experience of grace, mercy, and peace through Jesus Christ abundantly suggested. But in vain ; the hardened rebel made no sign of surrender. He was prayed for ; but there was no apparent answer to those prayers. He was taken to a friend's house, where kind-hearted, fervent Christian men prayed with him and for him. It was all to no purpose ; they might as well have spoken to the winds, or to the vulture hastening to the prey. He fled from the place ; he sought to escape from the very scene of the merciful efforts made for his recovery. It was at this time he enlisted. The soldiering affair was probably a desperate attempt to flee from the presence of the Lord, the sound of whose gracious steps seemed more and more to trouble the ear of the guilty fugitive. "There is no peace, saith my God, to the wicked." This "no peace" is frequently the precursor of a clear conviction of sin. Better, surely, is the painful restlessness, the growing misery that dogs the heels of many a sinner, than the fatal confidence which dreads no judgment, and hopes for a to-morrow as abundant in sinful pleasure as the present.

Henry returned from the army, released from its stern discipline, but not less bound than before by the terrible rigours of the devil's service. One night in December, 1861, as he was passing along Hyde Street, an obscure, out-of-the-way, back street, the attention of his companions was drawn to the cheerful sounds of praise issuing from a little room. They beckoned to him to come on. "Hallo!" he exclaimed, "what's up?" To play a practical joke on him, they replied, "Lots of drink and fun." The sound of the hymn-singing fell pleasantly on his ear, and he could not resist a sudden impulse to go in. The place was crowded, and he was compelled to take his stand upon the stairs. The people, consisting of factory men and women, were gathered together for prayer and the Word. Revival grace and blessing had reached that poor, benighted back street; some were rejoicing with "joy unspeakable and full of glory," newly found in believing; others, deeply moved, were ready with bursting heart to say, "Sir, we would see Jesus;" and the audience generally were in good heart for hearing the Gospel. Edward Usher and two Christian brethren were conducting the meeting. The singing over, the reading of God's Word followed. It was the parable of the Prodigal Son. The speaker, in his comments, dwelt on the words, "Bread enough and to spare, and I perish with hunger." The preacher, little knowing that the very prodigal was listening to his words, described such a case as

Henry's. The picture was well drawn ; the reckless youth was forced for once to look into a mirror that reflected his own face in hideous, but too true, outline and feature. He felt constrained to recognize the likeness ; his heart smote him ; he said to himself, " Harry, thou art the man ! " One word above all others pierced him ; that word was "JESUS." It was the Holy Spirit. A sense of guilt, piercing and intolerable, seized upon him as he stood on the stair ; and such a tremor shook his soul that he was fain to catch hold of the banister to prevent his falling.

His first step was to return to the house of his father, who received him in love. Here, however, he found no rest ; the great Father's house was not yet reached, a terrible wilderness intervened. In his misery, he one day rushed out of the house, without his coat, and sought a neighbouring tavern, where he attempted to drown the voice of an accusing conscience in the intoxicating cup. But in vain. The drink seems to have lost its wonted potency; the more he drank, the louder did conscience raise its voice. He found he could not intoxicate himself, though he drank all day. Sometimes, in the case of an intoxicated man, sudden impending calamity has been known to produce immediate sobriety. Thus the enslaved and down-trodden soul re-asserts her power in a majestic and extraordinary manner over the tyrant appetites of the body. So, the conscience of Henry Moorhouse, quickened to a sense of sin, apprehensive of approaching judgment and eternal doom, refused to be silenced by the infernal spell of strong drink ; and by its awful authority maintained a sobriety in the soul, in spite of deep potations, such as in ordinary circumstances would surely have produced the most abject stupor of drunkenness.

A conscience awakened by the Spirit of God, is a movement of Divine power scarcely less stupendous than the resurrection of a man from the dead. There are, however, qualms of conscience, agitations in the breast, and disturbances of false peace—common operations of the Spirit, as the old divines would term them—that may be quenched in strong drink or otherwise. Soothing the nerves, cheering the heart, resting the brain, aiding digestion, by means of intoxicating liquors, is often nothing else than a self-deceiving method of excluding unpleasant reflections and of obtaining quietness of conscience. Coarse enough is the strong drink solace ; it seems to be the broadest grin of irony with which the devil mocks a soul fevered in its sins.

And yet it works no greater havoc in the end than the more refined sops in which other consciences find their rest and hope. The last novel, the gay party, the whirl of business, some political excitement, a thousand petty passing interests, furnish many with all the peace they ever know, the only relief from the ghostly memories that haunt their souls. Or it may be alms and charities, professions and devout performances, good resolutions and solemn vows, the tears extorted from nature by way of a promise to "pay all," or a compromise cunningly effected, as supposed, betwixt the world and Christ, like an arrangement among creditors, a compounding at so much as the estate will allow, or some one of the many other shifts which the sinner, too proud to accept the offer of free and unconditioned grace, is wont to make. But whether it be drink or devotion, it is all the same in the end ; that end is hell.

For three weeks he continued in this state, seeking rest and finding none. Sometimes he went to the Circus meetings, where he heard of the Name that is above every name, but he found no peace. His convictions deepened, and he sought in various ways to drown his misery. But

the misery would not drown; this misery never drowns.
His wretchedness always returned with increased intensity;
the host of malignant and tormenting demons went on
multiplying. Was there any chance for him? Unbelief
answered "No!" He was too far gone; his day of grace
was past; the Almighty could not do otherwise than punish
such an one. Despair suggested the most fearful and
wicked alternatives. "Go back to sin; nothing else is left
you; take your fill of it; 'twill be all the same in the end.
Or else, put an end to your miserable existence at once;
plunge into the unknown; nothing can be worse than this;
anything else might be better." So he reasoned with himself; now denouncing himself, now denouncing his fate,
now wishing he had never been born; again softening a
little, trying to pray, listening to wise counsels, and almost
hoping for better things. But when those momentary
gleams had passed, his darkness deepened, his anguish
grew worse, "the pains of hell took hold" upon him, the
terrible temptation to suicide assailed him, and his friends
trembled lest his reason should finally give way.

Three hours of this has been more than many a soul
could bear. Henry Moorhouse had three weeks of it. He
was now learning one of the hardest and most necessary
of all lessons—the evil of sin, the bitterness of departure
from God, the madness of contending with the Almighty.
In vain did he seek some alleviation of his distress; in
vain did he resolve on some better course. He tried to
hide himself from God; but he found he could not hide
himself even from himself. The light of a holy Omnisci-
ence and Omnipresence shone around him, blinding him,
as the glory of the ascended Son of God blinded Saul on
the way to Damascus. It seemed to him the intolerable
glare of an eye that watched him, that found him out, that
transfixed him, that judged and condemned him. He

could go nowhere, but God was there. He could look at nothing that did not suggest the thought of an offended God. A whole age was crowded into this period of anguish and remorse; the dread and despair he now felt was such as to leave in his inmost soul ineffaceable impressions, memories that were his life-long teachers, and feelings that made him most pitiful and loving towards every sinful fellow-creature.

As Henry Moorhouse reeled along this pathway of sorrow, he fell into the hands of a wise and tender-hearted guide and counsellor. It was surely the good providence of God that found for him such a friend in the most terrible and critical hour of his need. Mr. Walter Caddell, whose hospitable house was open to inquirers for the way as well as to pilgrims on it, took Henry by the hand. Receiving him cordially into his house, Mr. Caddell exerted a kindly and soothing influence upon the distracted youth; and although he was not directly instrumental in leading him to the Saviour, he was used of God to hold up his goings at a time when reason often tottered under the load of sin, and a single false step might have plunged the unhappy lad into suicide and perdition.

One day he went to see a young Christian in the engine-room of John Rylands and Sons' warehouse. His friend received him joyfully. There is a marvellous freshness, sweetness, and quickening power in the light that shines in a young convert's heart. It is morning light, all the more beautiful by reason of the contrast with the shadows it is just chasing away. It is the first silver beam of the New Creation, and has in it the calm and rest of the first glorious Sabbath, when the Creator rested from His finished work. Better still, it shines with the ineffable serenity of the never-to-be-forgotten morning when the Lord arose, bringing out of His own grave the dawn of an eternal day. Young grace is full of dewy freshness, bounding energy, and triumphant song. If ever a man shall win a soul, it is then.

Henry found his friend rejoicing in the Lord. This did not mend matters; the contrast of his old companion's joy with his own load of anguish made him worse. For the young convert to tell of his own deliverance did Henry no good; to bid him do as he had done was like sheer mockery; to assure him of Christ's willingness to save him made no impression. Henry could not see it. Wisely, and doubtless under the guidance of the seeking Saviour, the young Christian drew his friend's attention to the very words of God. Turning to Rom. x. 8—10, he read, "The word is nigh thee, even in thy mouth, and in thy heart; that is, the word of faith which we preach; that if thou shalt confess with thy mouth the Lord Jesus, and shalt believe in thine heart that God hath raised Him from the dead, thou shalt be saved. For with the heart man believeth unto righteousness, and with the mouth confession is made unto salvation."

"Now," said the young teacher, "do you believe that? Do you believe in the risen Saviour, and that the work of redemption is finished, because Christ is risen?"

"I do, with all my heart," replied Moorhouse.

"Then are you going to confess what you believe?"

"Of course I will," was the ready answer.

"What then?" said the other, pointing to the words, "Thou shalt be saved."

Henry trembled with a strange emotion.

"Oh," he cried out, "I see it! I am saved!"

He saw, he believed, he rejoiced, he confessed, and he was ready from that hour to bear witness for Christ there or anywhere else.

So simple, so easy! say some. Too simple, too easy!

say others. When the Holy Spirit teaches, it is always simple, always easy. The Lord can use even a blundering teacher and a mangled text. His own blessed word He is wont to use, and that, too, in a manner which unsanctified reason is not able to comprehend. Sinners are not saved by mere syllogisms on Scripture : yet God reasons with them thus, " Come now, and let us reason together, saith the Lord : though your sins be as scarlet, they shall be as white as snow; though they be red like crimson, they shall be as wool." That is good logic, for it is " the wisdom of God unto salvation to every one that believeth."

Awakened on a staircase ; converted in an engine-room ; found of the Spirit in a poor, little, vulgar meeting in the very unconsecrated ground of a back street ; bound to the Lord in the bonds of the everlasting covenant in a noisy place of busy toil ! It is the old story of Divine love and power rising superior to the petty circumstances of human wisdom and pride. The locality is nothing, the instrumentality is nothing ; the reality is everything ; the Lord Himself is all. Cathedral service or cottage-meeting ; inquiry-room or engine-room : it is all one, provided only there is a true union of sinner and Saviour—Jesus cordially accepted, and the sinner giving himself back in hearty surrender. Where in all the world shall the blood of Christ be of none effect when it is applied? What day, what hour of the revolving year, shall this one word fail, "Believe on the Lord Jesus Christ, and thou shalt be saved "? Jesus found Matthew taking custom at a toll-bar, the woman of Samaria at the well, James and John among the nets, the man possessed by demons among the tombs, Zaccheus among the branches of a sycamore-tree, the thief upon the cross, the Ethiopian eunuch in a chariot, Saul of Tarsus on the Damascus road, and Lydia by the river-side. Everywhere, in all sorts of situations, the Lord, when on earth, sought and found His own. I know not if, in His ministry in the flesh, Jesus found any sinner, or was found of any, in the Temple. He whipped the unholy traffickers out of their unlawful trade, but He could not whip them into a holy life. They were past all good, whether by whipping, or weeping. Yet that the riches of His grace may be known, He Himself tells us how the broken-hearted publican found the justifying God of mercy even in that " den of thieves," the Temple. The question of the inquirer should not be, " Where shall I find Him ? " but " Where shall I not find Him ? " The question of the soul-winner should not be, " Where shall I win a soul ? " but " Where shall I not win a soul for such a Saviour ? "

A friend tells how on one occasion, shortly after his conversion, Moorhouse grew pale on meeting certain of his former companions in the street. It was some time ere he recovered his wonted composure. He then explained that his old associates were men of character so desperate, he feared they would take his life. His covenant with them was a covenant of death; his agreement was with hell. Out of such depths did the grace of God bring this young man ! Is not this a brand plucked from the fire ? And yet the difference betwixt one saved man and another is comparatively a small matter. In the man of good morals it is nothing less than grace that saves ; in the man of deepest shame it is nothing more. Vice is detestable ; morality even without God is, in many ways, advantageous to men ; the poorest morality is infinitely better than the least vice. But so-called good works before conversion are no more the cause of the saving change, than the bootless toils of a benighted traveller are the cause of the sun's rising, by whose dawning light he finds the way.

The difference between one sinner and another is only a question as to the quarter of the pit where the perishing man was found. It may have been a cleaner corner ; but it was in the pit. It may have been nearer the centre or nearer the side, more in the light or more in the shade; but, all the same, it was in the pit. If a man is drowning, he is drowning much the same whether it be in six fathoms or in sixty. If one is saved solely by the self-sacrifice of another, it will be a poor boast that his neighbour was perishing in foul water, but himself in clean. Truly, the salvation of any sinner is a marvel; the salvation of such an one as Henry Moorhouse is a marvel of marvels. The sum of the matter is, Grace is sovereign, Salvation is free !

CHAPTER III.

New Life.

"And they began to be merry."—LUKE XV. 24.

LIVING Christianity is, of all things, practical. It is so, because the Spirit of Christ in the believer creates a tender conscience; and a conscience, purged and sweetened by the quickening power of the Holy Spirit and the peace-speaking blood of atonement, is the true spring of upright-ness and honour as in the sight of God. Work, honest work, must ever follow genuine conversion. It may be ruling a kingdom or trundling a wheel-barrow, sitting on the woolsack or making sacks to hold wool, brain-work or work that needs no brains, building a St. Paul's or cobbling old shoes, reforming a nation or sweeping a kitchen; in any case, the Spirit of life in Christ Jesus will be manifested in hearty and faithful service. The Lord's vineyard is wider than church or chapel, Sabbath-school or Mission-hall, prayer-meeting or Bible-reading; it is as wide as earth with its ten thousand honest occupations, and it means not only coming to Jesus, but also Jesus coming to every human relation, every worldly interest, every word and deed of life in the flesh.

"What is wrong with your shoes?" said a pastor's wife to her guest, a minister who was assisting her husband in evangelistic services. Surveying his boots with a curious air, the other replied, " It seems to me as if your servant-girl has been rubbing up my shoes with grate and fire-iron polish; they are glancing so bright." " I will tell you all about that," said the mistress. " Don't you know that Betsy was converted at the meeting last night, and she is just brushing the shoes with all the warmth of first love?" Yes; first love is warm, and it should always be practical! it should go into first works, and glance brightly in the very drudgeries of every-day life.

"What good does your religion do you?" demanded a furious carter, whose cart had got into collision with a neighbour's in one of our narrow streets. " I will tell you one good thing it does me," was the reply of the Christian carter, who took calmly the flourishing and cracking of the angry man's whip ; before I was converted I needed a new whip every year, but since I was turned to the Saviour, seven years ago, one whip has served me all the time, and it is as good as ever." That is practical Christianity ; it even goes into a carter's whip.

Henry Moorhouse was now a new man ; old things had passed away, all things had become new. Immediate separation from evil companions and all dishonourable courses, was the unquestionable result of his conversion. "Whatsoever things are true," says the Apostle Paul to the Philippians, "whatsoever things are honest, whatsoever things are just, whatsoever things are pure, whatsoever things are lovely, whatsoever things are of good report; if there be any virtue, if there be any praise, think on these things." To some of us who knew Moorhouse only in his latest years it seemed as if he had made those lofty Christian rules the constant and successful study of his life. His first outset in the path of well-doing is attested by those who knew him well.

Entering into partnership with his former companion,

Thomas Castle, now, happily, a fellow-Christian, they began business on the joint capital of three-pence. Betaking themselves to a " swag-shop," that is to say, a shop where hawkers are supplied with such articles as thread, tape, scissors, etc., at wholesale prices, they invested their small store of cash. By great diligence, and owing mainly to Henry's talent for business, by the end of the week they had thirty shillings each after paying all expenses.

Castle, having no turn for business, left his companion, and found employment in a saw-mill, meanwhile taking part in open-air preaching, and bearing a powerful testimony to the grace of God, who had changed the prize-fighter into a humble wrestler for the prize of life eternal. His career was cut short by an accident in the mill, resulting in his death. " Tom, my lad, art thou going to die?" said his sister to him, shortly before the end. " No, Hannah," he replied, with a smile, " not going to die ; going to live ; for he that believeth on Jesus shall never die." So he fell asleep.

Meanwhile, Henry entered into the employment of a shop-keeper in Oxford Street, Manchester, where he further proved his talents as a salesman. His master, he soon perceived, was over-stocked, and Henry suggested that the surplus should be sold by auction. To this his master objected, on the ground that the auctioneer's commission would swallow up the profits. In his zeal for his master, he offered to take out a license, pay for it, and sell the goods himself. This he did, commencing to auction in another shop his master had in Deansgate. Here he was most successful in selling, and greatly pleased his employer. Prosperous in business, prospering in spirit, he pursued an honourable course of Christian virtue, and was beginning to realize more and more the blessedness of the man whose character is pourtrayed in the first Psalm. He was now the tree planted by the rivers of water, and his leaf was green.

The following letter illustrates the change in the character of Henry Moorhouse, and reveals the joy and zeal of the young convert :—

"My dear brother in our risen Jesus—My soul is this morning filled with great joy, and I can to-day break forth into singing, and repeat—

> "'Above the rest this note shall swell,
> My Jesus hath done all things well.'

"Bless His Holy Name, He has done so. If, my dear brother, you had been with me last night, you would have been grateful to Him for His great mercies to us. He, last night, showed me that it was 'not by might, nor by power, but by My Spirit.' We had a glorious meeting in Fairfield Street ; the room was crowded to excess, and the power of God was felt right into our hearts. The blood of my dear Jesus, God's own Son (oh, is it not a happy privilege to call Him my Jesus ?) was washing away the unbelief of many sin-sick souls last night, and I know that many will spend a happy Christmas that would not have done so, only for the grace of my dear Lord and Master, Jesus Christ.

"After the meeting was over we were requested by some friends to go and see their father. We went, I and Tom and Mr. H——, and when I was introduced to him the old man wept and said, 'Oh, Harry, I knew thee when thou wast so very wicked, but I am glad to see thee so altered.' We retired into the parlour, and there the power of the Holy Ghost fell right upon us. We had prayer together for a dear young man that was there that wished to give his heart to God, and, when we were praying, the old man began to cry out, 'Lord Jesus, help me !' We wrestled with God for about half an hour that He would drive away the clouds of unbelief from around his heart, and the old man was crying bitterly, and he said, 'Oh, Jesus, what shall I do? Thou hast given me everything in this world that I could desire ; and what have I given Thee in return ?' We told him to give Him his heart, and, while we were praying again, the old man shouted out, 'That's Jesus—I see Him, I see Him ! glory be unto His name ; I am saved through the blood !' And the old man began to pray.

"Shortly after his wife came in, and he said to her, 'Oh, Mary, Mary, God has forgiven me my sins; I've seen Jesus on the cross ; I've felt the precious blood in my heart ; and I feel so happy : I must tell everybody what the Lord has done for me.' And then the old man began again to praise God for His mercies unto him. Oh, glory be unto His Name, He is, indeed, making bare His arm amongst us. The blood of my dear Saviour has not been shed in vain. Calvary has not had its victim for nought. Satan has not had his head bruised for nought. Glory be unto Christ's holy name, He will bring us safe to glory in spite of all in earth or hell, if we will only be faithful unto Him ! Oh, may God bless you, my dear brother, and put you close to the precious blood of my dear Saviour Jesus Christ.—H.M."

The conversion of Henry Moorhouse was sound and thorough. But no work of regenerating grace, be it never so profound or complete, exempts from subsequent conflict. The shores of the Red Sea may resound with the sweet song of redemption ; but the wilderness lies not far ahead. So with our young convert. His joy was full ; but he soon discovered in the cup of his happiness drops of the old gall of bitterness. Although his peace was like a river, the rocky bed of the deceitful heart quickly disturbed its even flow, and turned the peaceful stream into an angry torrent.

When Robert Annan of Dundee,* in the triumphant hour of conversion, imagined, like many another young convert, that sin would not much trouble him any more, great was his horror one day to find, as the result of sore provocation, the old habit of profane swearing threatening to return upon him, an oath almost leaping from his heart to his mouth. Annan, happily, was equal to the occasion. Putting both his hands upon his mouth he gagged himself effectually, being willing to seem a fool rather than sin. This child-like method of self-control he continued to employ, till, at length, the renewed will was strong enough to need the aid of the willing hand no more. Thus grace obtained the victory.

In like manner, Henry Moorhouse learned to distrust himself and maintain a strict watch at every avenue of the soul. On one occasion finding himself in the wrong, he did not conceal the matter or palliate the offence. Promptly and with perfect candour he confessed his fault. This he did, too, in the presence of some to whom he was an utter stranger. " I am a Christian," said he, with much feeling ; " and a Christian should ever love his neighbour as himself, and do to others as he would have others do to him." This afforded him an opportunity of bearing a testimony to the Saviour, who had done so much for him. His frankness, his evident sincerity, the testimony he bore to Christ, and the high calling of the sons of God, as well as his self-diminishing confession, made a deep impression on all present, some of whom were moved to tears.

This child-like transparency, this self-denying candour, this manly readiness to confess a fault, he constantly set himself to cultivate, and found it an effective means of promoting peace of mind and growth in gracious character.

* See " The Christian Hero ; A Sketch of the Life of Robert Annan." Morgan and Scott Ld.

At first, amidst the joys and triumphs of faith, he had almost lost sight of the "old man." Bitter was his sense of humiliation when he discovered sin lurking in the thickets of his heart, and ready to spring a surprise upon him. War between the flesh and the spirit he saw there must be, and he began to gird his loins for the conflict.

The first stage in the Christian course is, in many respects, the most important. It gives tone and complexion to all that follows. Our young convert was now laying the foundations. He had found the way to his closet, and he had learned to shut the door. He was much in prayer, and by habitual exercise was gradually rising to an eminent post on the watch-tower. Exuberant though his joy was, he found it did not exempt him from conflict. Nay, the more grace abounded, the more urgent seemed to grow the necessity to watch and pray. The more grace, the more cross; the more blessing, the more battle. The bitter memories of his former life, the humbling experiences of his first Christian days, the sense of his weakness, the dread of sin, the constantly increasing knowledge of his own heart, and of Satan's devices, led him to frequent deep searchings of soul, and a jealous watching of himself, with the never-to-be-omitted prayer, " Lead us not into temptation, but deliver us from evil." His constant watchword was—

" My soul, be on thy guard ! "

At home, in the house of strangers where he sojourned, on entering into any company, on going forth to public duty, he could still be heard saying, " O my soul, be on thy guard ! " To watch and pray is doubtless one of the best accomplishments of the good soldier of Jesus Christ; and this he now cultivated with never-wearying diligence.

As one result, it was touching to hear him with mingled solemnity and tenderness addressing young Christians on the perils of temptation—temptations everywhere and in all things : temptations from within, from without, and from beneath ; that is, from the heart, from the world, and from the devil : temptations in the body, and temptations in the soul; temptations in speech, and temptations in silence ; temptations in work, and temptations in rest ; temptations at home, and temptations abroad ; temptations in society, and temptations in solitude ; temptations in health and in sickness, in prosperity and in adversity, in joy and in sorrow, from enemies and from friends : to self-trust and to despair, to shame and to undue boldness, to procrastination and to precipitancy, to carnal security and to unbelieving fear : in short, temptations in everything—"the greatest temptation out of hell" being, as Samuel Rutherford has said, "when there is no temptation."

This watching unto prayer more and more moderated his joy, toning it into that evenness and cheerful serenity of spirit which is the loftiest and safest condition of the soul outside of heaven.

It was at this period, too, that he acquired the habit of searching the Scriptures with prayer for light. More than anything else, perhaps, this practice was the spring of that stream of living water which brought refreshing to thousands in subsequent years. At first he renewed his strength by prayer ; by-and-by he happily learned to conjoin the Word with prayer, thus making communion complete. "Open Thou mine eyes, that I may behold wondrous things out of Thy law," became the motto of his spiritual life. He spoke and listened to God alternately, now putting his mouth to the trumpet of prayer, and then putting his ear to the trumpet of the Word. When he came upon a passage of Scripture he did not understand, it gave him much concern. He would read, ponder, pray, search the Bible, comparing Scripture with Scripture ; and when at length dawning light rewarded his persistent labours, he was wont to rejoice like one who had obtained a great victory, and secured much spoil. On such occasions, as his friends will readily remember, he would come out of his room, exclaiming, in tones as jubilant as those of the ancient philosopher, " I have found it ! I have found it ! "

In this way he put on his spirit that fine edge which was his chief characteristic as a Christian teacher ; and thus, too, he acquired the habit of maintaining the same fineness of edge, the loss of which is often the effect of much public work, and is the ruin of usefulness. He kept the grindstone in his closet on which he whetted a sickle that only grew sharper with the years. He fed his soul on truth and love. Thus he learned to keep the flame of personal love to his Saviour burning on the altar of his heart. So it has ever been with holy men and powerful preachers. Augustine was wont to break out in his preaching thus : "Oh, unspeakable love ! oh, sweetness of mercy inconceivable ! oh, most amazing condescension ! that God, for the sake of man, should be made man—that God for man should die in the flesh—that He should submit to be ' tempted in all things like as we are,' only without sin ! . . . . Let thy soul embrace thy crucified Jesus ; let it drink deep of His most precious blood. . . . . And oh, let this wonderful love take possession of all the love thou art capable of !" In like manner, Samuel Rutherford would exclaim, " He, He Himself is more excellent than heaven. Oh, what a life were it to sit beside this Well of Love, and drink and sing, sing and drink ! " So Henry Moorhouse with trusting heart would sometimes say, " Oh that I could die for Jesus ! "

This persistent course of close walking with God he continued to pursue after he entered into a quiet little home of his own. His marriage took place in October, 1870. In his early devoted friend Mary, he found a true Christian "help-meet." In full sympathy with him in his soul-winning, his wife smiled her blessing on him as he went forth on frequent journeyings and to distant fields. When he returned he found his house not only a haven of rest, but a sacred retreat, a school of Bible-study, a prophet's chamber on the wall. So we find him writing, "I do not forget the days, long since past and gone, when you, and you almost alone, tried to win me from a life of sin to Christ. And if the Lord has put honour upon me in making me a servant of His, I feel glad, darling, because I have you to share it with me. I am just longing to be back with you, love; you spoiled me for long trips by making our little home so nice. I find no place like it anywhere, and I get home-sick when I am away about a week."

In his own home he sought and found the discipline he needed for personal holiness and public service. In the course of the years his prayers for greater nearness and likeness to his Lord were answered in a manner he had little expected. He found a rare and most effective teacher in the person of his little paralyzed daughter, Minnie. In conversation with a friend on the subject of parental responsibility, he said he was not afraid, if it were so ordered in providence, to bring up a large family for God. Years afterwards, the same friend, meeting him, said, "How about the large family, Harry?" To which he replied, "My heavenly Father knew what was best for Harry. He has given me one little paralyzed girl; and she has done more to soften my heart for other poor little children and their sorrows than a crowd of healthy ones could have ever done." The sufferings and helplessness of this child, her words and ways, supplied him with endless illustrations of grace and truth, always instructive, and often beautiful. For instance, when speaking on the words of promise, "I will help thee; yea, I will uphold thee with the right hand of My righteousness," he said, "I have a little child at home, seven years old, paralyzed from babyhood, who, seeing me with a parcel I wanted to take upstairs, said, 'I will carry the parcel for you, father.' 'How can you carry the parcel, Minnie?' I asked. 'Ah,' replied the child, 'I will carry the parcel, and you will carry me!'"

He was by natural temperament affectionate and tender-hearted; yet, no doubt, it was in the school of his little daughter's sufferings that his spirit was touched to the singular fineness of feeling and gracious sweetness which, in his later years at least, were the predominating features of his character and preaching.

"I remember one time," he says, "I got down-hearted, cloudy, and dark. It was a very miserable day; at least, I was miserable. I do not think Christians ought to be miserable, no matter what kind of days there are. But so it was with me. It was Christmas Eve, and there was a thick fog all over Manchester, where I was; and the miserable sleety rain was coming down. I looked at my watch, and it was about eight o'clock. Four miles away there was a little cottage, with a bright fire and a nice cup of tea ready for me. I thought to myself, 'I will get right home, and make myself comfortable.' But at that moment I thought of a little child two miles away. There were no 'busses, and no trams—I should have to trudge all the way; and it was Christmas Eve. I began to think, 'Well now, little girls will want to have a doll to-morrow; I wonder if anybody has taken anything to this little child. It will be eleven o'clock before I get home if I go; and what will my wife say to my going home so late? And I will have to walk through the rain, and the slush, and the fog.' Something whispered, 'I would not do it if I were you.'

"But then another thought came: 'Suppose that child were your little Minnie, and there was no one to give her anything.' I went into a toy-shop, bought a doll for a few pence, and started off through the cold and the wet. By-and-by I came to a cellar, where this child lived with her mother and little brother. I knocked at the door, and a voice said, 'Come in.' I put my thumb on the latch, and went inside. There was a miserable little bit of fire burning, and no candle. By the light of the fire I saw the little boy sitting on one side; and lying on the bed there was the little girl, about nine years old. She was suffering from a terrible disease ; she was going to have her little leg taken off in a few weeks. She said to me, 'I am so glad you have come ; nobody has been to see us ; and mother has gone to see if she could get anything to do, and get some money to buy the Christmas dinner with.' I said, 'I have come to give you a doll ;' and I gave it to her. The little thing looked at it ; then she put her hand into the bed, and took out some old rags. She said, 'I have been trying to make a doll myself, but I have got a real one now.' She took the doll I gave her, and kissed it.

"In a moment the darkness had gone from my spirit ; the cold, chilly feeling had disappeared ; and I was as happy as ever I could be. I would not have missed taking that doll, that only cost threepence or fourpence, for a five-pound note. How glad it had made me ! And the next day the happiness I had in seeing my own little girl was ten times more, because I knew another little girl was made happy too."

"My dear little girl," he writes from America, in a time of storm and shipwreck, to his daughter Minnie, " what a world of sorrow we live in ; don't we, Minnie ? It will soon be Christmas now, and I wonder if my little girl would like to try and make somebody happy that day. I wonder if Minnie would like to buy Mrs. C—— a Christmas dinner, and to send her little cousins (Uncle James's boys) a nice

Christmas-box each ?   Minnie has money of her own, and
Papa would be so glad if she would of her own accord do
these things.   I have no money, or else I would do
it; but I am sure Minnie will—won't you, my pet ?   So
with love to all at home, and praying God to bless my
darling child, and all in Stretford.   " H. M."

This earnest desire and endeavour to train his little girl
in self-sacrificing works of love shows how full his own heart
was of Christian kindness.   And yet he says his Father in
heaven had taught him by his paralyzed child more than
he could teach her, more than he had learned by other
means.

His "newness of life" was early fostered by holy associations and friendships.   His conversion was in all respects
a distinct, clear-cut separation from the world.   He went
clean over to the Lord's side.   There was no halting, no
reservations in the interest of the flesh, no attempts to
mince the matter, or maintain some secret, sly, or slender
connection with the world.   He started well.   He identified
himself with the most spiritually-minded men, the most
thoroughly-devoted Christians, the most apostolic, self-
denying, and disinterested soul-winners, the most decided
and outspoken friends of true revival.   He loved them.
He loved their company, their zeal, their much prayer, their
heroic bearing of the cross, their holy ways.   But for this
he might never have appeared on the field at all.   Men
possessing gifts and grace, sometimes, from a timorous,
worldly-wise policy, fearing what is called "extremes," which
is really only a closer imitation of Christ than the world
likes, shrink into themselves, and shrivel into an utterly
unprofitable religious profession.   Moorhouse was enabled
to take a stand, and to share the offence of the cross with

the men whose zeal and faithfulness scandalized the tem-
porizers ; and the cross brought him the holiest friendships
on earth, advanced him to high usefulness in Christ, and
the honour that comes from God.

Thus all his relationships were revolutionized. That
this tree was of the Heavenly Father's planting became
apparent to all men from the fruit it bore. From the first
in Henry Moorhouse could be seen " the fruit of the Spirit,
which is love, joy, peace, long-suffering, gentleness, goodness, faith, meekness, temperance." Clearly this was a new
creation : old things had passed away, all things had become new. The more hideous the old, the more beautiful
seemed the new. It was a marvel, a lesson, a gospel to
look on the two Henrys—Henry the first by flesh and blood,
and Henry the second by the grace of God. Nor did the
stamp of "newness," as in the case of too many young
converts, become dim with age ; so did he walk with God,
it grew brighter and brighter with the advancing years.

CHAPTER IV

Work in England and Wales.

"Son, go work to-day in My vineyard."—MATT. XXI. 28.

HENRY'S heart aglow with all the ardour of a young convert, it was meet he should bear a testimony to the grace of Him who had wrought so great a work on him. Under the guidance of his friend and counsellor, Mr. Caddell, an opportunity was found. A large room in Walter Street, Ancoats, had, at the suggestion of some working-men recently converted at the Alhambra Circus, been taken by the gentleman just named for the preaching of the Gospel. Here two young ladies had gathered together some three or four hundred young women, for the double purpose of making garments for themselves, and of hearing about the garments of salvation. To this company Mr. Moorhouse delivered his first address. It may encourage some timid apprentice in Christian work to know that this his first attempt was a comparative failure. Often a good candle burns but dimly at first. The very cause of failure is sometimes the spring of success. Good is the diffidence that drives us to Christ; strong is the weakness that waits on the Lord. Ignorance of the Scriptures enfeebled Henry's testimony; but by the urgent and oft-repeated advice of his friend he gave himself to the prayerful study of the Word. Had he spoken less feebly, he might have gone on without his friend's counsel, and missed that which became the chief feature of his teaching, the very crown of his evangelism—his rare insight into the Word of God, and his power in handling it for the instruction and edification of at once the most illiterate and the most intelligent in any Christian assembly. A glib tongue, "a fatal facility of speech," has impaired the usefulness of many a beginner; while the humiliating failure of others has led to faith and prayer, to power and success.

Not long after, it was proposed by the same friend to gather together in the Walter Street room as many thieves and other bad characters as could be induced to attend, for the purpose of hearing from Henry Moorhouse an account of his conversion, and a plain statement of the way of life. To this Henry agreed, and a large number of the lowest class were invited to tea. To each was given a printed card of invitation, in the following terms :—

NONE BUT THIEVES, ROGUES,

AND VAGABONDS, ADMITTED.

Some four hundred attended; there was an enormous consumption of victuals, and a terrifying noise. Henry failed to appear. Probably the remembrance of the past, not less than inexperience as a preacher, unnerved him. The meeting was addressed by Mr. Harrison Ord; and many, melted into tears, professed a desire to forsake their evil ways.

Henry's business began to give him concern. The stock was largely composed of Birmingham trinkets, and the question arose whether the puffing of such articles was in strict keeping with the profession and duty of a Christian.

His conscience became more and more uneasy. Relief came in a curious way. One day as he was busy selling, and doubtless indulging a good deal in the rattling wit of the profession, J. B., an eccentric character, a weird prophet-like man who wore no hat, and went about everywhere warning men of judgment to come, entered the shop and cried out to Henry, "Thou ought to be with thy Bible for souls, and drop that hammer for the devil." It was a word in season. This was what he felt in his conscience. He thought he heard the voice of God in it. He left the business, not however in any dishonourable manner, or with any loss to his master, and went forth to preach the Kingdom of God.

In the early days of his Christian course Moorhouse came under the influence of Mr. John Hambleton, whose genial sympathies and ripe experience greatly helped him. Together they visited cities, towns, villages, and unfrequented rural parishes, preaching Christ as they went. Strangers, not always regarded with a friendly eye, and sometimes in want of every comfort, they bore up bravely amidst many discouragements, enduring hardship as good soldiers of Jesus Christ. Now and again, their wants were providentially supplied, and they felt that the watchful eye of their gracious Master was on them. Best of all, doors of usefulness were opened, and as they preached Jesus many believed.

In Halifax they found a remarkable opening. A work of grace was in progress, and it was given them largely to reap of its fruits. Night after night the Odd Fellows' Hall was crowded ; and many of the people, both old and young, were moved to tears by the simple and touching words of the boy-like preacher. Many, it is believed, were then "added to the Lord."

The young evangelist's first love had not abated, and his

soul overflowed with peace and joy.   So close was his walk with God that in sleep his lips moved in audible praise and in rapt fellowship.   " Precious, precious, precious Lord Jesus ! I praise Thee, O Lord !   And I believe in faith that works for the Lord—faith that works.   We want more love to Thee, Lord, and to one another.   Lord, help us to walk humbly before Thee ; to walk honestly before Thee ; to walk truthfully before Thee—redeeming the time because the days are evil."   Again, " It is a blessed thing to know that God keeps us, and it is a blessed thing to know that He does a great deal more besides.   Thank the Lord ! Thank the Lord ! Thank the Lord !"   These and other like expressions his companion heard him utter in his sleep.

In want of a text for one of his boards, Mr. Hambleton was supplied with suitable words one night as he lay awake and listened to Henry's talking in sleep.   " There I stood with a board, on which was printed, ' Christ for me ! Christ for me !' and the poor people were singing so happy." Then adding, " Praise the Lord ! Mercy's free !" he ceased and slept on quietly till morning   So " Christ for me ! Praise the Lord ! Mercy's free !" became the simple gospel of the new board.

In Scarborough they preached in a theatre, enjoying much blessing in the work.   Here many professed faith in Christ, some of whom are preaching the gospel to this day. Leaving that town, they pressed on to various towns and villages, proclaiming salvation through the Lord Jesus, with the usual results, the glad reception of the message on the part of some, and the sad rejection of it on the part of others.   Here they encountered difficulties, there they met with persecution ; but they endured as seeing Him who is invisible, and went on rejoicing in their great Master, until they arrived at the scene of the Shakespeare Tercentenary, at Stratford-on-Avon.

Here they were joined by Mr. Edward Usher, who brought with him a large supply of Bibles, Testaments, and Tracts. It needed high courage to face the excited crowd who had gathered from every quarter to celebrate the birth of the great poet. These did not want religion just then and there ; and to be confronted by three simple men of God with their Bibles and boards was truly more than weak human nature in the circumstances could have been expected meekly to bear. Four hundred London professionals fiddled and sung, " He was wounded for our transgressions ; " but that was a totally different affair, for while the prophecies of Isaiah and the holiest truths of revelation afford delightful entertainment when accompanied with first-class music, gospel texts borne aloft by the hands or uttered by the voices of redeemed men, is not agreeable to the carnal mind. " Sirs, it just comes to this in the end, Heaven or Hell? If you don't come to Christ, you won't go to Heaven when you die !" is much too grim a form of the gospel to afford amusement. It need not, therefore, astonish the reader to learn that the people gnashed with their teeth, tore the tracts and threw the fragments in the faces of the evangelists, and otherwise indicated the offence of the Cross with sufficient plainness. But they persevered in bearing their testimony to the truth : nor did they go without the rich reward of souls won for Christ. Going over to Shottingfield, they were followed by hundreds of the local peasantry, who listened with delight to the gospel, and in instances not a few were brought to the Saviour.

Passing on to Epsom they boldly raised the standard of the Cross amidst the wild excitements of the race. Nothing daunted by the rude jostling of the angry crowds, the raillery, the blasphemy, and the ferocious use of the horse-whip and all sorts of missiles, they preached Jesus and left the issue with their Master. To pass through such scenes is, to a fine, sensitive nature, scarcely less than the martyr's fire. It was an ordeal demanding strong faith, invincible courage, and quenchless zeal. But such cross-bearing service never fails of success.

From Epsom they proceeded to London, Bristol, and other places, with varied experience, but never without signs of their Master's presence and some happy indications of His blessing. Thus slowly they made their way back to Manchester.

Henry Moorhouse's evangelistic labours were now incessant. Doors opened on every side; nor was he slow to enter. The "boy-preacher," as he was called, began to be more and more sought after, the interest in his preaching, often raised by mere curiosity, not seldom leading to conversion. In company with Edward Usher, he visited Oldham, Rochdale, Liverpool, and Chester, where, during the races, they delivered fifty thousand tracts in three days. Passing over the names of various places, where faithful service in the Gospel was rendered, and precious fruits gathered into the garner of Christ, we next find Mr. Moorhouse and Mr. Usher in Dublin. In the Irish capital they were warmly received by Mr. Fry, and the lamented Mr Henry Bewley, with whom our evangelist formed a friendship of the most affectionate and enduring character. Here, and in many other parts of Ireland, a wide field of opportunity seemed to be providentially prepared for the young English preacher.

As usual, at first, his diminutive stature and boyish looks raised a prejudice against him; but his unaffected simplicity of manner and the soul of genial affection that animated his style quickly disarmed criticism: the quiet, gentle, insinuating power attending his addresses almost without fail carried his audiences with him. Imperfect though he was in knowledge, and sometimes crude enough in doctrinal statement, for he had not yet completed his evangelistic apprenticeship, his humble ministry was plainly stamped with the broad seal of heaven. The Holy Spirit used the fire of his zeal to kindle a corresponding flame in the hearts of many believers, and to communicate the first mysterious spark of spiritual life to many who had been, till now, dead in trespasses and sins.

In the theatre at Cork he and John Hambleton encountered a fierce, tumultuous mob of Romanists, whose too evident purpose was to prevent the preaching a free and full salvation through faith in the atoning blood of Christ. By yelling and other hideous noises and threatening demonstrations they succeeded in drowning the voices of the preachers. One strange song they sang,—" We'll hang Garibaldi on a sour apple tree." But they did not, save in figures of speech, hang the evangelists, who by dint of that national courage that does not know when it is beaten, persevered until victory crowned their peaceful arms; and Mr. Hambleton was enabled to deliver the message of salvation.

From the time of his first visit to the Green Isle, Mr. Moorhouse was established in the hearts of the warm Christian people of that country as a Heaven-born preacher of the Cross. Sweetly and tenderly, yet without compromising one iota of the truth, he was enabled to preach the Gospel in a manner all his own, to old and young, to rich and poor, to learned and illiterate, everywhere diffusing a savour of Christ, and seldom without some marked spiritual result. Welcomed to the drawing-rooms and saloons of the great, he never lost his head, or forgot his place, or left his Master downstairs. A favourite with the soldiers, he knew enough of their life to be able to touch a spring of tenderness even under the red-coat, and frequently they were melted into tears. One very memorable address, among the last he gave in the neighbourhood of the Irish capital, was delivered at Black Rock. He happened on that occasion to be utterly at a loss for a suitable theme, when, in his extremity, his thoughts fixed on the text, " Let the inhabitants of the Rock sing," from which he discoursed with characteristic freshness and power,

As a specimen of the evangelizing work carried on by Mr. Moorhouse the following is selected from the records of that period. Assisted by Edward Usher and Joshua Poole, he laboured for some time in the worst parts of Dublin, known as " The Liberties." In this quarter live thousands of the poorest and most debased people in the Irish metropolis ; and hitherto little had been done to carry the gospel to them. Services were held in the old Congregational Meeting-House with very remarkable results. At the meetings held by our evangelist and his fellow-workers, the attendance rose from fifty to thirteen hundred, many being Roman Catholics, with not a few of such as had never seen the interior of any place of worship. Great power attended the word, and many professed to believe in Christ.

At the first meeting a young man, stepping in from sheer curiosity, took his place among the audience. He was deeply impressed. For the first time his eye lighted on the invisible cross of the gospel : he saw, as he had never seen, the atoning sacrifice, the risen, loving Saviour. He believed and wept for very joy. His first step was to hasten home and tell what great things God had done for him. Next night he brought one of his sisters, who, smitten with conviction of sin, remained to the second meeting. Taken in hand by a lady, she was instructed in the knowledge of God's way of justifying sinners. It pleased God, by His Spirit, to bless the truth : the scales of unbelief fell from her eyes, she saw Jesus as the Lamb of God, and believing, went her way home rejoicing. At next meeting the brother and sister, now one in the Lord, brought another sister, with the burning desire and confident hope that this one also would, that very night, be numbered with those who are washed in the blood of Jesus. And so it came to pass, for she, too, was found of Him who came to seek and to save the lost. Unspeakable was the happiness of sisters and brother in this new and better family bond. Yet one remained; their mother was not in Christ. Deeply concerned about her salvation, much prayer was offered on her behalf, and every effort made that tender love could suggest. For the meeting on the following Friday night extraordinary prayer had been made, and with the usual result when the Holy Spirit is thus breathing in the souls of believers. There was a breaking down of hearts, many were weeping, and seeking the Lord ; among the rest that mother. In the meeting for inquirers she found rest in Christ and began to rejoice with somewhat of the joy that is unspeakable and full of glory. Her son, hearing of what had taken place, entered the chapel, where he met his newly-saved mother. A touching scene was witnessed. Mother and son, meeting in the aisle, fell on each other's neck and wept. Thus a whole family was saved.

Nor was this a solitary instance of the kind. Quite a number of entire families were believed to have entered the ark at this time. It was a memorable season. The hearts of believers were wonderfully stirred, and it seemed as if eternity had been disclosed to view. The evangelists were full of joy and power. For their encouragement in the work of Christ the following verses were written by a Christian lady :—

" Onward, onward, brothers ! onward !
There's a glorious prize in view ;
Though the way be rough and thorny,
God will ever guide you through.

Take the sword of His own Spirit,
  And with helmet on your head,
Be ye strong in Jesu's merit;
  Think—for you the Saviour bled.

" Onward, onward, brothers ! onward !
  Do not linger by the way;
Say to dying sinners round you,
  ' Jesus calls to you to-day.'
Tell them what He is to you,
  How He loved, long, long ago !
Tell them how He rescued you
  From the depths of endless woe.

" Onward, onward, brothers ! onward !
  Soon your warfare will be o'er,
Soon you'll cast your armour from you,
  Landed on fair Canaan's shore.
There, amid the ransomed throng,
  You shall swell the note of praise,
And with loudest, sweetest song,
  Sing of Jesu's matchless grace."

The following letter, which appeared in " The Revival "
of April 13, 1865, lays bare the secret of his power :—

" DESIRE—PRAY—BELIEVE.

" It is now about a year since the Lord gave me faith
to trust entirely upon His arm, and to leave all for the sake
of Jesus.   Since then I have visited many places in Eng
land and Ireland, and in some little measure the Lord has
blessed my labours.

" Beloved brethren in the Lord Jesus, especially those
brought to a knowledge of the truth during the last twelve
months in Bradford, Halifax, Scarborough, and Chester,
I wish to impress upon you the necessity of much prayer.
This desire has been placed in my own soul by hearing

the Lord speak by Richard Weaver, the other night, in Dublin.

" When the Lord made me happy in Jesus, about three years ago, I spent every night either in prayer or praise. But after a little while my desire for prayer cooled down, and I was content to pray twice a day. The Lord in mercy revived his work in my soul, and now my desire is to pray always.

" What precious promises are given to every one of us! and it is by pondering on what the Word of God really promises that we are led to act upon that Word. The Word declares that ' what things soever ye desire, when ye pray, believe that ye receive them, and ye shall have them.' (Mark xi. 24). Now, there is large scope in these words; the Lord Jesus has not restricted us to any particular object. But whatsoever ye *desire;*—first there is to be a desire, and I believe the Spirit itself places that desire in our souls ; and then we are to pray, for the Lord will be inquired of ; and then we are to believe, and all things are possible unto them that believe.

" Beloved friends in Christ, have you a desire to see the Lord's work revive in your town or family? Would you like to see sinners crying out for mercy and made heirs of glory? Do you desire to see the arm of the Lord awake, and miracles of mercy wrought in this your day? If so, thank God there is the *first* thing, ' what things soever *ye desire.*'

" Now Christ said, ' what things soever ye desire *when ye pray.*' When and for how long ought I to pray? is the next question. Did not Jesus say?—' Men ought always to pray ; ' and He gives us examples, such as the widow and the unjust judge, the man and his friend. ' Pray alway,' means whenever I can get a moment with the Lord : at my work ; in the house ; at home or abroad ; on my knees or on my feet; in my bed or at my business; pray always, and faint not, for in due time we shall reap.

"When ye pray, plead and wrestle with the Lord for that which is upon your soul, whatsoever it may be. If it be a revival of the gospel, pray for that. If you desire the conversion of your relatives, pray for that. Whatever good you really *desire*, pray for. There is no limit to your prayers if the things asked for be really desired.

"But the words of our Lord are, 'What things soever ye desire when ye pray, *believe.*' The blessed Lord gives us whatever we desire when we pray, upon *one* condition. That condition is faith in Himself. The desire may be burning in our hearts, and we may pray alway, and never faint ; but the Lord has not promised to give us our desires for praying, but He is bound by his own Word to give us our desires if we pray *believing.* God cannot deny Himself, neither can He deny his Word, and if any of the Lord's children, however unworthy, have the two requisite conditions—first the *desire*, and then the *faith*, and obey the injunction *pray*, God will surely hear, and in mercy answer.

"I ask your prayers for myself, and for all the dear labourers in the vineyard of Christ. May God give you a desire to pray, and faith to believe, that He will use us for his honour and glory. DESIRE—PRAY—BELIEVE.

"H. MOORHOUSE."

CHAPTER V.

Work in America.

"Say not, I am a child; for thou shalt go to all that I shall send thee."—JER. I. 7.

ON the wide American field it was given Henry Moorhouse to gather many sheaves for his Master. Here, more even than in his own country, his labours were sealed by the Spirit of God. Within the limits of a brief narrative it is impossible to follow him in all his movements, or to enter into the details of his work in any one place. Nor is this necessary, if it were possible. Dipping here and there into his life-work will suffice to furnish a fair specimen, a suitable illustration, of the whole.

His six visits to the New World were fruitful of blessing ; but perhaps his first American tour yielded far richer results than any other period in his evangelistic ministry. He went there, a stranger in a strange land, in much fear and trembling. At the outset he encountered difficulties that might have appalled a stouter heart than his. His faith was sometimes sorely tried ; his tender susceptibilities were deeply wounded. But the same hand that emptied the vessel also filled it ; and the emptying not less than the filling was the work of grace. A wide and an effectual door was opened for him. He was honoured with invitations from churches and cities; he was welcomed with enthusiasm, and hailed as "the great English preacher:" thousands hung on his lips, and, infinitely better than all, the Holy Spirit accompanied his preaching with great power; whole congregations were moved to tears and inquiry, and many were added to the Lord. It was given him, especially at this period, not only to hold up before many thousands the Great Picture, but also—O rare grace!—himself to stand well out of sight, while with solemn tenderness he said, "Behold the Lamb of God!"

Some extracts from his diary of this first visit to New York supply an interesting record of experience and service:—

"JESUS ONLY.

"*New York, Sept.* 7, 1867.—A stranger here, without a friend! Nay, Henry, 'there is a Friend that sticketh closer than a brother;' and He who cannot lie has promised never to leave nor forsake thee; so do not doubt, only believe, and all will yet be well.

"Just seventeen days since the *Virginia* (Captain Prouse) sailed from Queenstown—six hundred steerage and fifty-seven saloon passengers, myself among the number. It was a happy time; the Lord enabled me to preach Christ to nearly all on board, the Dutch included, and I am sure there was blessing. The Lord be praised! The tracts were thankfully received, and many asked me for the 'Words of Comfort.' I saw many sights I shall never forget. One poor mother, with a grown-up daughter, very, very sick; and how she nursed her! Oh, who on earth is like a mother? I think if I were dying, I should like no hand to smooth my pillow save my darling mother's, no kiss upon my lips save the kiss of her that nursed me when a child. Lord, make me to value more Thy love, and the love of my sweet mother! At last the child got better; and how sweet the smile upon the mother's lips! I spoke about the Saviour to them both, and the tears started to their eyes as they heard about the precious atoning blood of the Lord Jesus Christ.

" I found out that the daughter had been married two days before the vessel sailed, that the father had been in America about six months, and had sent for them ; and so mother, daughter, and son-in-law were going out to the father and husband. After paying their passage money they had not a sixpence left.

" I don't think I can write much about the voyage, save that I formed a friendship with Dr. Samuels of Liverpool, the ship's surgeon, and another gentleman, likewise from Liverpool, the latter a very dear Christian, and the only one on board I had communion with about heavenly things.

" Well, it seemed a long passage, but *at last* we sighted land. The tears came quickly into my eyes as I jumped ashore. I don't know why ; perhaps 'twas a foretaste of the sorrow I must endure in this strange land. Why call it strange ? 'tis like the world everywhere when left to itself. A Republic. Everybody seems to think he is better than everybody else, and it is hard to get a civil word from anybody. Well, give me my country, and my beloved Queen, and never again will I grumble at Monarchy. This is a dear place—ten shillings for a coach to bring my luggage to the hotel, five minutes' journey ; fifty cents, or two shillings, for hair-cutting and shampooing, and everything else about as dear in proportion. Went to Castle Gardens, the emigration offices ; found my three English friends in deep sorrow; no money, and don't know what to do; want to get to Boston and can't ; no train to-day. Took them to a cheap boarding-house ; three dollars a day for me to pay for them out of my scanty purse, which feels very light at present. Well, I do it to the Lord, so never mind; He will look after me.

"I see two things here in my bedroom I never saw before in any hotel : first, mosquitoes, which I really don't like, they bite so bad ; the second, a Bible, presented by the American Bible Society. I suppose they have given one for each room. Well, blessed be God, I love the dear old book, and rejoice to see what they are doing here with it. So now, my dear boy, read a chapter, say your prayers, and go to bed, for I'm sure you must be tired. God is love, and He giveth His beloved sleep.

"*8th.*—And so Lord's-day is over, and not without its lessons either. Surely God is leading me by ways I know not ; but 'tis blessed (is it not ?) to be sure in one's soul that He knows and He never makes mistakes. No ! He is wise and He is kind.

"Broke bread to-day—a happy time ; went to a Methodist Sunday-school and had a little cry as I heard them singing, ' Work while 'tis day.' In the evening went to a church and saw the ' mark of the beast,' as in England. Well, God any-way will take care of His Church, whatever England does with hers.

"My word, Henry, but you have walked many miles to-day, and your poor feet are sore ! Don't it make you think about Samaria, and the well, and the woman, and the blessed, blessed holy Jesus ?—Tired !—what, He weary ? Ah yes ! and yet He never murmured, because 'twas the path of obedience. Well, Henry, learn of Him ; obey His commands—do good to all men ; 'twill soon be passed ; life is but a vapour, and time passeth swiftly ; the Lord has blessed you, Henry, and will again ; learn to be content— God bless you !

"*Friday Evening,* 13*th.*—How time flies ! have been here now nearly a week ; don't care much for New York ;

Christians seem all dead. Fulton-street Prayer-meeting to me seems not the right thing. People don't read their Bibles, I am sure, or they would never have such erroneous doctrines. Told them it's dreadful to sit and listen to a man telling us that if God don't punish us here He will hereafter. Well, the dear old Book that cannot lie tells me He (Christ) was punished for mine, and I believe it.

"And so the poor people cost me near twenty-five dollars! Well, 'twas well spent; any way you will never be any poorer for what you have done, my boy, in the name of the Lord.

"Had a nice ride to-day from New York to Philadelphia; passed along the Delaware river, saw the floating timber, and much pleased with the country. Got a good hearty welcome from Mr. and Mrs. Porter, and begin to feel at home, at last. *Home* I long for. Work! Lord, help me to work while it is called to-day.

"*14th.*—Met dear Mr. Porter to-day, glad to see me, took a walk out, and then he told me he believed in the annihilation or total destruction of the wicked, body and soul. That put me in a fix, for I believe this is a dreadful heresy, and so I refuse to break bread with him.

"Well, what's to be done now I don't know: three thousand miles away from home, and only twenty dollars left. Well, never mind; God is my Father; the Lord is my Shepherd; the Holy Ghost my Comforter; the Word my guide. ' I will never leave thee nor forsake thee'; only trust.

"Mrs. and Mr. West are very nice and kind, and Mrs. Graham very full of love. Called to see Mr. Campbell— out; his wife just got a telegram to say Dr. Inglis could not come to preach; did not know what to do. Here, says she, the Lord has sent you; and so at last, Doctor, I am to have a meeting in America. The Lord be praised! I do hope God will give me souls for Christ Jesus.

"15th.—Happy time to-day breaking bread, the Lord present. Spoke from sixteenth of John to Christians. Preached to-night, not so much liberty, but hope there was blessing.

"26th.—Have since I last wrote in my book been able to preach Christ almost every evening. Met many kind, beloved friends, among whom I mention Dr. and Mrs. Reid, with whom I now stay, Mr. McCollins and wife, Mr. Towrie, who has given me his church to preach in for a week. Not much to say except I find it ploughing work, but shall surely reap, if I faint not."

As he went on itinerating, Henry found some in every place who received him cordially, and entertained him with true American hospitality. The feeling of the "stranger," the slight home-sickness he felt at New York, gave place to a sense of rest, enlargement in his preaching, and remarkable results in the conversion of sinners. From Philadelphia he went to Melville, and Camden ; and to Pittsburgh, where he preached in the theatre to great crowds, and with much power.

In December we find him back to Philadelphia, which he left on the 11th, with much tenderness on parting with his friends. "Left to-day," he writes in his journal, "the hospitable roof of beloved Dr. and Mrs. Reid, Philadelphia. The tears were in our eyes as we said Good-bye, and I felt it hard to go away. How very kind they have been to me since I came a perfect stranger to their city ! They took me in, lodged, boarded, nursed me when a little sick, and took care of me, and altogether were like beloved parents unto me. Truly the Lord will bless them."

From that city he passed on to Wilmington, State of Delaware, where he was kindly received by Mr. William Hills, one of the Society of Friends. In his diary he proceeds to tell that—

" After supper, Mr. Shaw, Presbyterian minister, called to take me to the meeting. It was a bitterly cold night, and the hall being too small to hold the people, they had to adjourn to the church, which was nearly filled. The minister gave out 'Rock of Ages,' and read part of the twenty-third of Luke, and then offered up a very fervent prayer for blessing upon the meeting. He then introduced me, and I gave out the hymn ' All hail the power of Jesu's name'; after which I preached from these words : 'Through this Man is preached unto you the forgiveness of sins.' I had not much liberty, but felt great power. All paid great attention to the preached word.

" *Dec.* 12*th.*—Went to-day to the meeting of the Society of Friends. After sitting for a time in silence, I felt led to preach, which I did from John iii. 16, and had a very sweet, refreshing time and great liberty, and much of the felt presence of the Lord. In the evening went to a meeting for coloured people, and had a very happy time, preaching from the words, 'Walk worthy of God.' I like the coloured people very much ; they are so honest and truthful. Ask them if they are Christians, and at once you get the answer yes or no ; I like to see the intense desire they have to learn to read and write. At the meeting to-night I noticed a middle-aged woman, who paid great attention and said 'Amen ' now and then. After preaching, I went to shake hands with her, and I found she had with her a copy-book, and slate and arithmetic. I examined her writing-book, and found she was only in pot-hooks and hangers. ' Oh,' said she, ' I do lub Jesus better than all the world beside. He lub me and die for me, and I am His, for eber and eber.' As she spoke her eyes filled with tears, which rolled like pearls down her black happy face, and grasping my hand, she said, ' God bless you, sir ! ' I felt I was repaid for preaching as she said those words. Now may the blessed Saviour make Himself known to many hearts is my prayer to-night !

"13*th*.—Went this afternoon to the coloured day-schools —very interesting time. Spoke first to the boys, who seemed very bright and intelligent; sang very loudly. To the royal proclamation; spoke to them, gave them little books. Then went to the girls' school—spoke to them; they also sing very sweetly; gave them books also. Mr. Shaw spoke to them. Mr. Hills accompanied me to the meeting in the evening in the Methodists' house; power with the word.

"21*st*.—The goodness of the Lord to you, Harry, is beyond description. What doors He has opened ! What friends He has raised you up ! What blessed opportunities to preach the word ! What power, and what blessed results ! Beloved Mr. Hills—how happy he seems now !—so miserable before, going about like a man condemned; but now, by the truth, delivered from bondage and the curse. Well, go on; sow in the morning, Harry, and in the evening withhold not thy hand; thou knowest not which shall prosper, this or that. Now, what have you been doing all the week ? Well, bless the Lord, last Sunday morning went and preached at Grace Church (Mr. Shepherson, pastor)—a most fashionable, rich congregation. Text, 1 Tim. i. 15, ' Christ Jesus came into the world to save sinners.' God made me very simple, and the word was with power; indeed, many weeping, including the minister. After preaching, the people thronged around me to bid me God-speed, and I was asked to take a week's meetings down at the Mission Chapel among the poor, which I gladly accepted. In the afternoon at three, felt very tired and weak; preached in the coloured church from John iii. 16—'the love of God.' What a scene !— shouting, screaming, laughing, crying, and clapping of hands. But when the sufferings of Christ upon the cross were being described their eyes seemed fastened upon it. A long-drawn sigh they gave as one man, and others buried their faces in their hands. They sobbed aloud. It was a precious time—God with us in mighty power! When I had finished they thronged around me, and, with tearful eyes, shook my hands, or clasped me in their arms, and prayed, ' God bless and take care of you,' and said, ' Do stay ; we lub so much to hear what you say about Jesus. Bless de Lord ! bless de Lord !' It was very amusing to see them take the little books, which many could not read, but they clasped them to their heart, because they spoke of Christ. One said, ' Mine's very 'freshing '; another said, ' Mine's very 'taining ' ; another, ' Mine's like yours ' ; another said, ' They're all alike.' It's wonderful to see the eagerness with which this once down-trodden race learn to read and write ; old men and old women, as well as young, go to school and learn A B C, and so on, until at last they learn to read their Bible. I find much real Christianity among them, a very simple, child-like faith in Christ, a holy life and great devotion to the Saviour. Many of them are Methodists, but I find some Baptists and some Presbyterians among them. They are very intelligent. Thank God for the abolishment of that which cursed both slaves and their owners ! Blessed be God for the proclamation of liberty to poor sinners ! A glorious liberty He gives to all who trust His name.

" In the evening preached with much liberty and great power from the words—' the precious blood of Christ.' Here the arm of the Lord seemed made bare, and the word sank into many hearts. Had some of the richest people in the place there to listen to the Gospel. Glory be to God for ever, who often takes the poor, and the base, and the foolish to preach His faith and to win souls to the dear Saviour. After this day's work I came home tired, but happy, and with much of the assurance that I was in my right place and at the right work.

"*Monday.* — A beloved fellow-labourer, whom God has sent to me (James Field), in his visits heard that protracted meetings were going on at one of the coloured churches, and soon arrangements were made for me to preach. Went there in the evening; had a very crowded meeting; all coloured people, except James and I, and one or two more who came in. Blessed meeting, and great power. After the service the minister asked that the mourners would come forward, and about fifty men and women all fell upon their knees, the rest all standing, or sitting. About a dozen women, who I suppose were Christians, set about their work, helping these anxious ones to get liberty. First taking off their own bonnets and shawls, they very deliberately set about taking from the necks and heads of the penitents all their upper garments. Bonnets, head-dresses, shawls, neck-ties, ribbons, and brooches were stripped off and put inside the communion-rails, all the time singing a very lively hymn. Then the minister asked a brother to pray, which he tried to do, but I, who was next to him, could not hear him. Such shouting, and bawling, and stamping, and clapping, among the bystanders; and weeping, and crying, and screaming, among the penitents! Then another hymn and then prayer again. I came away and left them shouting 'Glory, Hallelujah!'

"*Tuesday Evening.*—Advertised to give a lecture on the 'Work of an Evangelist,' or my own experience in the Lord's work. Place crowded—-Presbyterian; almost every denomination represented. Great power; much weeping, and an attention in Christians rarely seen. Have seen fruit from that blessed meeting.

"*Wednesday.*—Again in the Zion coloured church. A

good attendance; very quiet, solemn time; much liberty. Preached Jesus as the Friend of publicans and sinners.

" *Thursday Evening.*—In another coloured church, and again God manifested His love to sinners and His power through the preaching of His precious name. At the close they again gathered round me, and wished me soon to come and preach again to them, and I said ' good-bye ' with a heavy heart, as, poor things, they need very much the preaching in its simplicity of the love of Jesus.

" *Sunday Evening.*—Preached again in Central Church with great help from the Lord. A very precious time. Spoke to anxious ones. God is doing a very blessed work in this city, I am persuaded, and in heaven I shall meet many brought to Christ during this visit.

" *December* 31*st.*— Since I wrote last in my diary, I have left Wilmington, and am now at Claymont, staying with dear Mr. Kimber, a very nice, benevolent man, one of the Society of Friends. A very handsome place in a delightful spot ; his heart is large and open. Well, I had altogether a very blessed time in Wilmington ; all the pastors so kind, especially Mr. Shaw, Presbyterian. I preached the sixteen days I was there about twenty-four times ; large meetings— so large towards the last the people could not get in to hear the Gospel ; and I saw much of the power of God. Everybody seemed to like me, and the word through me. I suppose ten thousand books were given out one by one by James Field. My English friends followed me everywhere. The scene in the almshouse was very touching. . . . .

" The power of God on Christmas Day was wonderful. A woman fell down upon her knees and cried out for mercy. Mr. Shaw brought me twenty-eight dollars as a token of love, and said ' I shall send you more.' Promised to go back for another week. Preaching the last night there from the words 'Turn ye.' Very solemn and much power. Stayed to watch-meeting; happy, peaceful time."

Mr. Kimber, here referred to, an eminent minister among the Friends, gives the following interesting reminiscences of Moorhouse :—

" More than thirteen years have passed since he came, one cold winter evening, with a letter from a dear friend and brother, who was 'called home' before him; and I shall never forget how, on entering the hall door, he stood with his satchel in hand, at the threshold, and saluted me, as I went forth to welcome him, with the searching inquiry whether I were a Christian. It would be difficult to explain how distasteful and embarrassing this question was to me at that time; how repugnant to all our habits of thought and education on such matters; how all efforts to avoid, or even to postpone, his close inquiry were unavailing. He did 'not want to sit down to the supper-table,' which I explained to him was all ready; 'the Lord told me first to inquire if the master of this house were a Christian, before entering or partaking of his hospitality.'

" I found there was no other way than frankly to confess that, in the sense of an assurance of salvation, I was not one; but added that, by the grace of God, I would never say that again. It was enough; my strange guest entered, having done what the Lord undoubtedly sent him to me to do—broken the fetters which had held my tongue. A wonderful watch-night service, in the little meeting-house hard by, filled to overflowing and lasting for four hours, attested the remarkable powers of this new-comer amongst us to hold his audience with unflagging interest, as he told the simple story of the cross. I had always loved the Lord, even when wandering from Him; but for several years had been earnestly seeking to serve Him. The Holy Scriptures were regularly read in my family, with a season of silent waiting at the close ; but never had my lips been opened before others in prayer or praise, or confession of our needs, or of God's salvation. So it needed just such a faithful and uncompromising messenger, who would brook no delay or evasion, on his Master's errand, to bring me out into a measure of the liberty of the Gospel, although he could have known nothing of my condition.

" His power was marvellous over those with whom he came in contact. High or low, rich or poor, cultured or uneducated, all attended his public ministrations with the deepest interest; and all seemed to feel sure of a word in season from him, of sympathy or counsel, or of prayer, suited to their conditions, in more private intercourse ; so that all loved him, and many wept when he left us to go to Chicago, on his first visit to that eminent servant of the Lord, D. L. Moody, to whom he was ordained to be such a great blessing.

"I remember, on one occasion, a bright young school-girl, about sixteen years of age, came into the room where Henry Moorhouse was sitting, and seeing him with his Bible before him, was about to withdraw with an apology for the interruption, when, looking up with a loving smile, he said to her gently, calling her by name, 'Are you saved ? '

" For a few moments she stood silently, with downcast eye and grave face, blushing with confusion at the un-expected question, and then her sense of the real Christian interest which must have prompted it, overcame her natural dislike to speak of her personal experience, and she slowly answered, 'No, I am afraid I am not.' 'Would you like to be ? ' was the quick and gentle response of Henry Moor-house. Then came the great struggle of her life—as she still stood, silent and thoughtful, weighing the whole subject, once and for ever, whether she really would or not. The

world with its pleasures all around her; her young life with
its bright opening prospects all before her; some of her
friends; some of her pursuits; the enmity of her natural
heart to the Lord,—all these were on *one* side.   His Holy
Spirit gently pleading with her, and drawing her to her
Saviour, whom at heart she loved; his servant's mild,
earnest look of the deepest interest, fixed upon her, in this
supreme moment of decision, caught as she raised her eyes
timidly towards him; her pious mother's prayers; the
eternal interests of her immortal soul—*these* were all ranged
on the *other* side.

" Happily for her, these at last won the victory; and
softly, yet firmly, she answered, ' Yes.'

" ' Then kneel down at this sofa,' said Henry Moorhouse,
' for the Lord says, " To-day is the day of salvation," and
read aloud with me this beautiful story of what Jesus has
done for you (Isa. liii.), and take every word to yourself, as
you read it, verse by verse.'

" She did so, and the blessed truths of the Gospel, and
of her Saviour's sufferings, never seemed so real, and so
dear to her, as then, and her tears dropped freely on the
page she was reading.   The blessed Holy Spirit was doing
his work.   The Lord's promise of old, ' Draw nigh unto
Me, and I will draw nigh unto you,' is ' yea and amen in
Christ Jesus' for ever.   Our Saviour's own declaration,
' Him that cometh unto Me I will in nowise (no never !)
cast out,' is known to be a living reality by all those who
believe and accept it in simplicity and faith.

" When she had finished the chapter, Henry Moorhouse
said to her, ' Now begin over again, and read it once more
aloud, putting " *I*" instead of " *we*," and " *my*" instead of
" *our*," and just forget that it was written for any one but
yourself.   Read it as though you were the only person to
whom it applied.'

"It is a blessed thing to be persuadable in a right cause —to be 'easy to be entreated,' is one of the evidences of heavenly wisdom. Many miss the joy and peace that they might know, and paralyze the efforts of the Lord's servants to help them, simply because they refuse to give a trial to the means proposed, forgetting that the Holy Spirit uses instrumentalities, as well as works directly, in opening the eyes of the people.

"So she began the chapter, as he was led to suggest, reading it slowly and vocally, while endeavouring to appropriate its blessed truths to herself. And now indeed they seemed to shine forth as she had never comprehended them before, and coming to the words, 'But He was wounded for *my* transgressions ; He was bruised for *my* iniquities ; the chastisement of *my* peace was upon Him, and with *his* stripes I am healed,' the Lord's light and salvation broke upon her soul, and smiling through her tears, she looked up wonderingly and said, '*Am I healed?* Can it be that I am saved?' 'Yes, dear child,' Henry Moorhouse replied gently, as he beheld the seal of the Lamb on her forehead, 'that is just what Jesus has done for you'; and then he praised the Lord for another soul delivered, and redeemed by the precious blood of Christ.

"Let none who read this say that it was but a momentary emotion. The twelve years that have passed over, since she rose from her knees, with a new life and immortal hope in her heart, on that memorable day, have only deepened and confirmed her faith and reliance on that Saviour whom she found, then and there, to be precious to her soul ; and as a happy Christian wife for more than half of that interval she has cast her influence steadily both in her home and in her church on the Lord's side."

"*Thursday Evening.*—A very precious, powerful meeting. Upwards of fifteen prayed in succession. Much, very much, of God's presence, and I believe one rested upon Christ.

" *Friday.*—A good turn out, but much hindrance in the prayer-meeting. Some of the professors have taken a great dislike to the simple Gospel ; suppose the light shows them too much rubbish in their works, etc. ; but the Lord helps me to be faithful with them.

" *Sunday Morning.*—Heard an excellent sermon from a dear Methodist minister, Mr. Cunningham, on the words, 'Not every one that saith unto Me, Lord, Lord,' etc. Some of the people did not like it. Preached in the afternoon at a church. Good attention ; much power ; very simple, and after meeting many prayed for me. So different in the evening ! Text—'God so loved the world.' Much liberty and power ; but afterwards in the prayer-meeting much restraint. Found out the reason very quick. I saw at the close one of the class-leaders with a most diabolical look upon his face. I went to shake hands with him. He turned his back to me ; but I put out my hand and he took it.

" A young man came to me and asked if I was converted, and how I felt. I told him yes, and asked in return if he was. He said he had been once. He went on to say he saw sparks, blue flames, and felt something coming down, and it fell on him, and it ran all over him, and out of his fingers. I hear he is a backslider, so I suppose all his religion ran away from him. Well, I suppose the dear Lord will bless His own precious truth, and will take care of His seed scattered here. 'Tis a hard place—the hardest place I was ever in. Lord, help me ! Amen.

" *January* 15*th.*—The work here—at least my work for the Master—is, I am sure, finished in Claymont. The meetings have been well attended, and the Word of God has been preached ; many Christians have been refreshed, and some sinners made to think about their souls. Miss S—— has been brought to Christ. The dear Saviour help her! She is a very lovely, kind-hearted girl; I must always pray for her. Had a very nice pastors' meeting here on Saturday evening last: much of the Master's presence. Preached Sunday morning in the Baptist Church. Good meeting. Dr. Dickinson, pastor, seemed much pleased.

"Began on Monday evening a week's meeting in the Town Hall, Wilmington, chiefly for firemen and young men who never go anywhere else. Good, happy time, so far. The Lord will bless, I am sure.

"*February 4th.*—Been to Baltimore; many professed conversion; mother and son, very affecting scene. On to Washington. Very dead; preached twice; gave tracts to Congress; sent them to the President and another party, and to the prison Suratt.

"*March 22nd.*—Since last writing, have been in Claymont, Albany, Philadelphia, Chicago, and now in Wheeling, Virginia. Had a good time here. Preached to-day in an Episcopal Church. Crowded house. Used neither gown nor Prayer-book. Text—'Who loved me, and gave Himself for me.' Liberty and power. To-night in the first Presbyterian Church. Crowded—hundreds unable to get in."

An unutterable longing to win souls filled his heart wherever he went, and it appeared as if he seldom opened his mouth without some being drawn to the Saviour. As showing at once the blessed enthusiasm that filled his soul, and the child-like simplicity and susceptibility with which he was characterized, the following little incident may be given. In the house of an American family where he was residing, the members of the household assembled on Christmas morning to examine the gifts which, according to custom, had been presented to each in token of friendship and peace. The boxes or packets were well filled, the gifts were varied, and there was universal joy. One, and one only of all present had received no such token of love; the English evangelist could claim no Christmas-box as his. But, although this little circumstance had no earthly significance, except that he was a stranger in a strange land, the intensely affectionate and sensitive nature of Henry was moved to its depths. He thought of his own dear England far away, and of his loved ones there; and to conceal his feelings he retired to his own room. In the course of the afternoon, a man who had attended the meeting on the previous night, and had been convinced of sin, called on the evangelist, and ere the interview closed, was enabled to declare his faith in Christ, and to enter into joy and peace. "Ah!" said Henry, "the Lord saw that my heart was sad, and He gave me a Christmas-box Himself!"

Another incident will illustrate the success attending his labours on the American continent. Tidings of his power as a preacher having reached a certain town, an invitation was sent him by some of the leading people of the place. He consented to pay them a visit. On the day fixed for his arrival, a deputation of importance went to the railway station to receive and welcome him with all the dignity and formality that became the occasion. But "the great English preacher" was not to be found; or at least, no man answering to their conception of the powerful evangelist was anywhere visible. Hurrying out to the omnibus, they inquired if Mr. Moorhouse was there, when to their amazement a little, simple-looking, round-faced lad, standing on the steps of the carriage, with a bag in his hand, made reply, "I am Mr. Moorhouse." On this, the gentlemen of the deputation conducted him with due courtesy to the hotel, where they proceeded to read a solemn address of welcome. Pausing in the midst of the ceremony, the reader, glancing at the diminutive figure before him, and still doubting whether such a tiny morsel of humanity could possibly be the great preacher, whose fame had almost overspread a continent, inquired once more, " Am I correct in assuming you are Mr. Moorhouse ? " Again assured by the little stranger that he was the very man, the reader of the address proceeded, and this rare scene was brought to a close. In relating this amusing incident, Henry used to say he only wished his mother had been there to witness it. If any doubt as to the stranger's identity lingered in the minds of those good citizens, it was quickly dispelled, when in the public meetings the lad brought forward his little store of loaves and fishes, and his great Master so blessed the provision that a multitude was feasted and sent away rejoicing, and more seemed to be left for the next meal than was found at the beginning, for every basket was full.

In the course of this tour our evangelist visited Chicago. In the absence of Mr. Moody, he prosecuted his labours, preaching every night six or seven times in succession on his favourite text, John iii. 16. Pouring out his heart in a stream of gracious truth, apt illustration, and touching appeal, he proclaimed the love of God in Christ to a perishing world. The audience was deeply moved ; the people felt a heaven-born preacher had appeared among them. On his return, Mr. Moody went to hear and see for himself, and was much impressed, especially by the tender pathos of the preacher. In his enthusiasm he went and hired the Farwell Hall, and covered every space in the great city with huge posters, announcing in flaming capitals the celebrated, the wonderful English Boy Preacher. The vast building was crowded, and Moorhouse preached. The preaching was a complete failure, his tongue was tied. The audience waited in vain for something wonderful; there was nothing to be wondered at, unless it were the wonderful collapse. Moody was confounded. Not so Moorhouse, who, noticing on the way home one of the grand bills, exclaimed, "Ah, here is the explanation of our failure! Exalting man so! God could not bless that!" It says not a little for the moral courage of Moorhouse that instead of hastening away from the scene of so humiliating a failure, he went on calmly and hopefully with his work. The soldier who is too proud to fight after he is beaten is unworthy of victory. "Steadfast and unmoveable," our evangelist knew that his "labour should not be in vain *in the Lord.*" And so it proved to be.

On beginning his Bible-readings in this city, he requested the people to bring their Bibles with them. This they did; but for lack of more portable copies, some were seen entering the meetings with huge family tomes under their arms. As usual in his readings, the word fell like dew; the people were delighted and refreshed. To many it was summer in the soul. Thinking the charm partly lay in the copy of God's Book, handled with so much ability and freshness by the preacher, not a few expressed a desire to possess the same edition. This brought many copies of Bagster's Polyglot to Chicago. In this way Moorhouse put the Word of God into the hands of believers in Christ a second time; and the new light coming in with the new method was like a fresh revelation from heaven. And yet the new method was nothing more nor less than the intelligent and laborious searching of the Scriptures. It was in this way and at this time that the Chicago evangelist and other eminent American workers got on the track of Bible reading. Moorhouse taught Moody to draw his sword full length, to fling the scabbard away, and enter the battle with the naked blade.

CHAPTER VI.

The World for a Parish.

"Go ye into all the world, and preach the gospel to every creature."
MARK XVI. 15.

ON one occasion, at the close of an expository lecture, or
Bible-reading, a certain nobleman, impressed with a sense
of the little preacher's ability, generously offered to find a
parish for him in the Church of England, and to confer on
him a living. To this course Mr. Moorhouse pointed out
some serious obstacles. These, however, the large-hearted
nobleman assured him could all be removed. But our
evangelist did not see his way to confine his labours to a
field of so limited extent. Even this difficulty should not
stand in the way, for the earnest patron, happily, would be
able to secure for him one of the most populous of parishes.
"Ah!" said Moorhouse, "my parish is the world, and I
cannot give it up for anything less." Contented with the
patronage of Heaven, and the living his Divine Master
provided for him, Henry stuck to his parish.

In the mouth of Henry Moorhouse the famous saying
of Wesley was not the language of exaggeration. As far as
in him lay, he went into all the world, preaching the Gospel
to every creature. Throughout England, its large cities, its
towns, its villages, across to Ireland again and again, occasionally to Scotland, and six times to America he made his

way, Bible in hand, ever ready and eager to tell how "God so loved the world that He gave His only-begotten Son," or with heart-moving pathos to describe the Prodigal's return. In churches, chapels, schools, halls, tents, theatres, circuses, alhambras, public-houses, west-end drawing-rooms, miners' cottages, on the decks, in the saloons and steerage of ships, on the sea-shore, in markets, fairs, festivals, at race-courses, and in all places where men congregated, among soldiers, sailors, civilians of every order, from high nobility down to tag-rag, among drunkards, prostitutes, thieves, and all sorts of jail birds, he made his way with the Gospel banner in his hand, with no eloquence but truth, no motive but love, and no policy but the single eye to the glory of God. The man capable of doing this is, beyond dispute, the man sent of God to do it, and blessed in the doing of it.

As illustrative of his work and the blessing that often attended his labours, I will select two instances from very different classes of society. First, a young lady receiving the word. One night, he tells, a young lady came to me in the inquiry-room, and said, " Will you tell me what you mean by knowing that you are saved?" She was a member of a church and loved the Saviour, but did not know that she was saved. " Will you come and sit down here, and open your Bible at the fifth chapter of John, and read the twenty-fourth verse. She turned and read, " Verily, verily, I say unto you, He that heareth My word, and believeth on Him that sent Me." " Now," I said, " spell the next word." " H—a—t—h." " That is not hope," I said ; " that is *hath.*" She turned to me, a smile lighting up her face through her tears, and said, " That is to have everlasting life." " Are you saved now?" I asked. " Yes." " How do you know?" " Because," she replied, " it says so ; and that is how I know."

"We tell you to-night in the Master's name," he goes on to say, "you can be saved here if you are guilty—if you have nothing to give to God; for Jesus came to preach the Gospel to the poor. Some of you say, 'Mustn't I repent for a week or two; must I not try to get some of the sin taken from me and then go to the Lord; and when He sees I desire to be better, it will be easier?' My friends, you can't improve yourselves. He wants to take you just as you are."

The next is the story of a wicked Yorkshire collier, whose hard heart was softened by

"NOTHIN' BUT T' LOVE O' CHRIST."

"When I was holding meetings a little time ago at Wharncliffe, in England, a coal district, a great burly collier came up to me and said in his Yorkshire dialect, 'Dost know wha was at meetin' t'night?' 'No,' I answered. 'Why,' said he, 'So-and-so' (mentioning the name). The name was a familiar one. He was a very bad man, one of the wildest, wickedest men in Yorkshire, according to his own confession, and according to the confession of everybody who knew him. 'Weel,' said the man, 'he cam' into meetin' an' said you didn't preach right; he said thou preached nothin' but love o' Christ, an' that won't do for drunken colliers; ye want t' shake 'em over t' pit; an' he says he'll ne'er come again.' He thought I did not preach enough about hell.

"I did not expect to see him again, but he came the next night without washing his face, right from the pit, with all his working clothes upon him. This drunken collier sat down on one of the seats that were used for little children, and got as near to me as possible. The sermon from first to last was on 'Love.' He listened at first attentively, but

by-and-by I saw him with the sleeve of his rough coat
wiping his eyes. Soon after, we had an inquiry meeting,
when some of those praying colliers got around him, and it
was not long before he was crying, ' O Lord, save me.! I
am lost ! Jesus, have mercy upon me !' and that night he
left the meeting a new creature.

" His wife told me herself what occurred when he came
home. His little children heard him coming along—they
knew the step of his heavy clogs—and ran to their mother
in terror, clinging to her skirts. He opened the door as
gently as could be. He had had a habit of banging the door.
If a man becomes converted, it will even make a difference
in the slamming of doors. When he came into the house
and saw the children clinging to their mother, frightened,
he just stooped down and picked up the youngest girl in his
arms and looked at her, the tears rolling down his cheeks.
' Mary, Mary, God has sent thy father home to thee,' and
kissed her. He picked up another, 'God has sent thy
father home ; ' and from one to another he went and kissed
them all, and then came to his wife and put his arms around
her neck, ' Don't cry, lass ; don't cry. God has sent thy
husband home at last : don't cry ; ' and all she could do was
to put her arms round his neck and sob. And then he
said, ' Have you got a Bible in the house, lass ? ' They had
not got such a thing. ' Well, lass, if we haven't, we must
pray.' They got down on their knees, and all he could say
was—

> ' Gentle Jesus, meek and mild,
> Look upon a little child ;
> Pity my simplicity—

for Jesus Christ's sake, amen.'

" It was a simple prayer, but God answered it. While
I was at Barnet some time after that, a friend came to me
and said, ' I've got good news for you. So-and-so (men

tioning the collier's name) is preaching the gospel everywhere he goes—in the pit and out of the pit, and trying to win everybody to the Lord Jesus Christ.' Oh, brothers and sisters, will you not trust the Saviour? Dear mothers and fathers, will you not believe the gospel? Will you not rest upon that finished work? Will you not give up your doings and strivings, and just like a little child rest upon that Saviour? Believe the glorious gospel, and have everlasting life."

In August, 1869, he revisited America, accompanied by Mr. Herbert W. Taylor. A farewell meeting was held in Merrion Hall, Dublin, and on the following day they sailed in *The City of Washington* for New York. Here they remained only two days. Passing on to Philadelphia they remained in that city for nearly three months, holding services in various churches and chapels. After spending a few days in Baltimore and Wheeling, in West Virginia, they took their way to Chicago, where they stayed with Mr. D. L. Moody for a couple of months, preaching in his church and the Farwell Hall of the Y. M. C. A. During this time, accompanied by Mr. Moody, they went to Columbia, in Ohio, for a week, holding some seventy-two meetings in that time, amidst remarkable indications of divine blessing Leaving Mr. Moody, they went to Richmond, Indiana, where they preached the Gospel in the Friends' Meetinghouse. Joining Mr. Payson Hammond in special services in Cincinnati for a few days, they thence returned to Chicago.

In the end of January, 1870, they started for California, halting for a week at Rock Island on the banks of the Mississippi, which, at this time, was frozen over, the thermometer standing many degrees below zero. In this town and in Devonport, on the other side of the great river, they held meetings, the Bible lectures by Mr. Moorhouse being much appreciated. Thence to Omaha, where they spent a week before setting out on the long journey across the prairies westward to the Pacific. At Ogden, where they spent a night, they found sorry accommodation, the floor of the hotel being occupied by gold miners returning home with their treasure in their belts. On entering the room they heard the click of some fifty pistols—a hint scarcely needed by the messengers of peace. In a very tiny room they found a sleeping-place, where, for fear of being robbed, they lay with their clothes beneath their heads.

At Salt Lake City they preached twice to the Mormons, two of the bishops giving the use of their meeting-rooms. The meetings were crowded, many being unable to find admission. On their way across the Rocky Mountains and the Sierra Nevadas, the cold, rarefied air brought on bleeding of the nose and spitting of blood with Henry Moorhouse. On arriving at Sacramento they proceeded by steamer to San Francisco, where the doctor ordered the suffering evangelist to the warmer climate of San José, his companion remaining to preach in the great Californian city. Ten days at a farm-house in the beautiful valley of San José completely restored Moorhouse. Two days at San Francisco, and a week at Sacramento, they then started on their homeward journey, travelling from Monday morning till Friday afternoon a distance of fifteen hundred miles. After a brief stay at Omaha they proceeded to Chicago, where they spent another month of earnest service. Leaving the great city of the west they went by Detroit to London, Ontario, Canada, and from thence to Niagara, and down the beautiful Hudson. After paying brief visits to Philadelphia, Wilmington, and Baltimore, they sailed from New York in May, and, after a pleasant passage, reached home. This journey was full of work and of blessing, which, doubtless, the Day will declare.

Again we find our evangelist in America. In the winter of 1872 he conducted services in Chicago, crowds attending and much power accompanying the Word. At a meeting in the North Side Tabernacle he met Mr. Sankey for the first time. " His grand simplicity, power of illustration, and strong faith in God and in the power of His Word, caused me to look upon him," writes his last-named friend, " as one of the most powerful preachers of the Gospel I ever listened to." From this time they became warm friends, and held many meetings together. " It was he who first suggested the thought of going across the sea to sing the Gospel," says Mr. Sankey, " and I remember how confidently he expressed his opinion that God would bless my singing there."

After his return to England Mr. Moorhouse was among the first to welcome Messrs. Moody and Sankey at Liverpool, on the occasion of their visit to this country in June, 1873. At Newcastle-on-Tyne and at Darlington he assisted the American evangelists, taking a leading part in their first all-day meeting. Thereafter leaving them he proceeded to various places where he had appointments to preach.

The year following, 1874, finds him again on the other side of the Atlantic. On this occasion an extraordinary door was providentially opened for him at one of the University seats.

Invited to Princeton, Mr. Moorhouse preached in the second Presbyterian church (Dr. M'Corkle's) ; and, although it was at the time of an election, on account of which it was feared the meeting would be a failure, the house was crowded. Many of the professors and students from the college and seminary were present. The evangelist preached his sermon on "the blood," and such was the effect of the preacher's pathos and tenderness in showing that, " without the shedding of blood there is no remission of sins," that few eyes were dry. The Holy Spirit was manifestly present. Next night the crowd was even greater, and the power still more marked. A work of grace was begun among the students. Into this work Dr. M'Cosh, Dr. Hodge, and other professors, entered heartily, giving their countenance and aid to the pastors, and fostering the movement to the utmost. His lectures were specially appreciated and blessed. Mr. Frost, the gentleman whose guest he was and who had paved his way to Princeton, threw his house open to inquirers. The students in groups coming in a spirit of earnest inquiry, "sat at his feet, tearfully and joyfully" listening to his expositions of Old and New Testaments. "I never before so understood God's Word," one would say. "How clearly I now see Christ in the Old Testament!" another would exclaim. Said one, "Will you tell me, so I will understand it, how to read the Bible as you read it."

On Sabbath morning he preached his well-known sermon on "The Far Country." "Most vividly did he picture the wandering of the sinner from the Father's house and table," his kind host relates, "and then how tenderly and impressively did he, in the Father's name, call them back to forgiveness, to the old home and the feast! The scene that morning is past description. When, after sermon, he asked those who would set their face toward a loving and forgiving Father's house to rise, there was a moment of suspense, then slowly the congregation rose, and it seemed as though there was not a soul that did not breathe in earnest, 'Father, I come to Thee.'"

In the evening he preached in the first Presbyterian church to a large congregation, the galleries crowded with students. In this discourse he proclaimed the doctrines of grace, giving a striking and memorable illustration of "election."

How to study the Bible as the very Word of God, and how to teach it with power for the salvation of men, are burning questions ; and the Princeton students felt that this stranger was in the secret. His Bible Lectures in the mornings were attended by as many as one hundred and fifty of the younger men, while his discussions of Bible Study and Pulpit Preparation in the afternoons attracted on an average some fifty students in theology. To teach one student is to teach a thousand souls. Many of them, now pastors, acknowledge the benefit thus derived; the success of their ministry they gratefully trace to the light that shone from the humble lamp of the English lay-preacher.

The Lancashire lad at the high seat of learning, standing up, Bible in hand, to instruct the future teachers of the Church, was a curious enough spectacle. It looked not unlike a modern rehearsal of the Bethlehem shepherd boy advancing to battle against the giant with sling and stone. Christ still comes in the carpenter's jacket; happy is the man, happy the church, and happy the college, that is not offended. All honour to the learned men of Princeton, and to the manly young scholars who could bid welcome to a simple lay-preacher, whose only letter of commendation was the Holy Spirit's seal on his labours ! The clear conscience-rousing voice of the evangelist, the solemn cheerful stir of the genuine revival meeting, the quickened pulse of spiritual life, the vivid sense of eternal verities divested of all scholastic forms, supply the best antidote to the intellectual pride by which halls of theology are too often cursed and the life of churches destroyed. There is no place where cobwebs, and all clever, cunning spider works, are so apt to gather and grow as the hall of sacred learning. Spiritual deadness, the rationalising spirit, and the pride of learning, is the threefold evil that afflicts many a school of the prophets in our day ; and for this the only remedy is the fresh breezes of the Holy Spirit. When colleges and divinity halls are brought to the exact level, whether by levelling up or levelling down, of the upper room at Pentecost, the Church's brightest day will be at hand.

In the later years of his public life, Mr. Moorhouse occasionally extended his labours to Scotland. Twice in 1875 he visited Dundee under the auspices of the Young Men's Christian Association. His first visit was in the month of February. To pay him honour as an evangelist of some eminence, the directors and some other gentlemen connected with the Young Men's Christian Association, met for the purpose of according him a complimentary and cordial reception. In the course of his journey, when looking out at the window of the railway carriage, our traveller had come by the mishap of losing his hat ; and when he made his *début* his boyish and unimposing presence was not diminished by the circumstance that he wore a little round undignified cap. So " weak " was the evangelist in personal appearance that the gentlemen holding the levée were beyond measure surprised. They had pictured to themselves a large, broad-shouldered, deep-chested, loud-voiced burly Englishman, or at least a man of solemn, dignified, weighty personality ; and so, when the little man, not the bearded evangelist of the modern type with somewhat of a John-the-Baptist mien and wilderness air, but a simple-looking, beardless lad, made his advent, some of the company found it necessary to retire in order to indulge in a chuckle of irrepressible surprise.

His first address set matters on another footing. It was evident to all who heard him on that occasion that Henry Moorhouse was not a child in understanding, but a man of great spiritual power. Every public utterance, every private conversation, while he was in Dundee, appeared to be attended by a remarkable influence, and produced invaluable results. In point of fact, no evangelist has ever appeared in this town whose words left a more purely spiritual and permanently gracious effect upon that portion of the Christian community who are most warm in sympathy with the word and work of the Lord Jesus.

He was at that time in a state of extreme bodily prostration ; his sufferings, arising from chronic bronchitis, combined with a painful and alarming affection in the region of the heart, being incessant and all but intolerable. His medical adviser had given him to understand that a fatal issue of his two-fold malady was a question only of months or of a year or two at most, and that from the nature of the case the exertion of public speaking must certainly hasten the end. At every Bible-reading, and in every evangelistic service, therefore, the sword, furbished and ready, seemed to hang over his head ; yet he went on in the work with unabated ardour and jubilance of soul. To the kind remonstrances of friends, he invariably made reply, saying, " Please God, I'll go on."

While here he found a quiet resting-place and a cheerful home in the house of David Robertson, Esq., the devoted president of the Young Men's Christian Association, whose like-minded wife tenderly nursed their afflicted guest. Despite extreme weakness and nights of intense suffering he proposed a series of Bible-readings, to be held in the house. Accordingly three such services, attended by various ministers of the gospel, and others, were held at Union Grove, the subjects being " The Good Shepherd," " Peace," and " Separation." These readings were attended by an unusual sense of the Divine Presence, and, like his other and more public addresses, left an ineffaceable impression on the minds of not a few. A sense of the glory of the

Lord, a vivid perception of the beauty of holiness, an elevating and joyful fellowship, appears to have been the common experience. None then present can ever forget the reading on " Separation." It was one of his favourite themes ; and the man himself, in the high tone of his soul and gracious purity of his character, clearly embodied his own lofty ideal of separation in a manner too rarely witnessed among the saints. His very first utterance on this topic made a profound impression, the memory of which intervening years have not even now effaced. Quoting Genesis i. 4, " And God divided the light from the darkness," he struck a key-note of power, as he pointed out that the dividing of light from darkness is the grand work of God in the conversion and sanctification of a ransomed people. His thoroughness in grappling with the question of a holy separation from the world, and the faithfulness with which he presented this truth in all his public addresses, was all the more seasonable and telling, in that the recent movement had resulted partly in conversion to mere hymn-singing, and a kind of religion not dead to the world. From this reading the company dispersed under the influence of deep emotion, one, a godly pastor, taking his way to the house of an elder of his Church, to whom he communicated with tears the soul-moving impressions of truth he had received.

The illness of Moorhouse went on increasing, until, at length, his kind friends of Union Grove called in an eminent physician. Examination was followed by prescriptions, one of which took the form of an advice to cease from public speaking. To this, however, he only replied, " Please God, I'll go on." Advertised to preach in the Kinnaird Hall, he rose from his bed at three o'clock in the afternoon, and despite the remonstrances of friends, the suffering occasioned by his malady, and the intolerable inconvenience of a chest all sore from the external application of croton oil, he was resolute in fulfilling his appointment; he would go and preach the Gospel once more. Still he said, " Please God, I'll go on." So he went, and preached with freshness and power on his favourite topic, God's love in Christ to a perishing world. As John Newton said of Scott, the commentator, in similar circumstances : If to preach with a blistered chest, after a night's anguish from partial suffocation, were an essential qualification of a bishop, aspirants to that high office would not be so numerous as they usually are. Henry Moorhouse was a bishop by divine appointment. Called by the Head of the Church, ordained by God, and anointed by the Holy Spirit, he was sealed in his office by grace, sufferings, and success. The loftiest of all qualifications was his, a consuming love to Christ. Because he loved his Lord and Saviour more than all else, and could say, " Thou knowest all things, Thou knowest that I love Thee," he had received the commission, " Feed My lambs; feed My sheep." Passing along one of our streets one day and noticing an advertising bill with his name in large letters and the subject in smaller characters, he expressed a feeling of deepest pain, because, as he said, it was the way of the world to give to man the honour due to the Lord. A man of this stamp is the chosen instrument of God; his power is simply the power of the risen and exalted Redeemer in him.

In public he gave his readings on "the Lamb of God," and " the ' Comes ' of Scripture." His meetings in Euclid Street Chapel, where he gave his readings on " Ruth," were crowded by audiences as intelligent as any that ever assembled in this town to hear the Gospel preached ; and the impression appears to be as fresh to-day as it was then.

The directors of the Young Men's Christian Association

were desirous of securing the services of some "great man" for the opening of their new hall : but utterly failing in their purpose they invited Henry Moorhouse ; and to our evangelist fell this honour. The hall was opened with a Bible-reading. This was in May, 1875, the time of his second visit, when he conducted a series of readings and evangelistic services with marked indications of Divine blessing. In this way not a few among us received a new conception of the Scriptures. A new source of power was thus opened to Christian workers, who now joyfully acknowledge their obligation, under God, to the English evangelist for increased skill in handling the Sword of the Spirit, whether for personal sanctification, or for the work of winning souls. "Henry Moorhouse," says one of the most eminent among them, "taught me how to use my Bible." To teach the teachers, to lead the leaders, is given only to a master in Israel.

In 1877, Mr. Moorhouse again visited America, taking part in services held by his friends, Messrs. Moody and Sankey. With the latter he held meetings in St. Johnsbury, Vt., which were attended by many of the leading people of the State, including the Governor and his family. At Manchester, N.H., and at Providence, R.I., he preached with great acceptance and power.

In Rochester, Mass., a remarkable blessing attended the Word. His afternoon bible-readings were crowded out of the large lecture-room into the body of the church (Dr. Shaw's). In the evenings, this large building, the brick church, capable of accommodating some two thousand five hundred, was crowded, and many hundreds were turned away for want of room. To a greater extent than upon his first visit to this city, he reached the consciences of the impenitent, and many were led to take a decided stand for Christ. All classes were interested in the truth, and more or less shared in the blessing. From two to three hundred individuals attended the inquiry meetings. "The young love him for what he has done for them," one writes, "and the old love him : all love him, and he will ever find a warm welcome in this city."

This was his last visit to America, for although he entertained thoughts of returning, and settling there, it was otherwise ordered by the Master. His work "across the water" was now brought to a solemn and fitting close.

The following farewell address was delivered in Dr. Hepworth's church, New York, when Mr. Moorhouse took as his subject, "The precious blood of Christ" (1 Pet. i. 19).

From the book of Genesis right through to the book of Revelation, he said, we find God exalting the blood of His dear Son. Analyse the book of Genesis, and you will find there is far more said about the sufferings and the death of the Lord Jesus than about anything else. Peter loves to dwell upon what the Lord Jesus Christ suffered. There was a time when he thought the Lord Jesus Christ should not suffer, and die ; he looked for His coming to reign as King ; but after he had learned the precious truth of His death and resurrection, he loved to speak and write of it. In none of the other epistles, in the same space, do we find so much spoken of the blood. In the second verse of the first chapter we read, "Elect, according to the foreknowledge of God the Father, through sanctification of the Spirit, unto obedience, and sprinkling of the blood of Jesus Christ." Then in the twenty-fourth verse of the second chapter, we have the words, "Who His own self bare our sins in His own body on the tree." In this one epistle we read of Christ's blood or death eight or nine times.

The doctrine of the blood is no new thing. During the six thousand years now gone, it was preached by prophet and priest.

6

(Here the preacher reviewed the earliest notices of the doctrine in Paradise and at Abel's offering).

In Genesis viii. 20, we have the beginning of a second dispensation. And it is remarkable to notice here that the first thing Noah did in coming out of the ark, was to shed blood.

Again in Exod. xii. we see the same truth concerning the precious blood. We find here that God just looked upon the one Lamb. Although throughout the vast congregation of Israel, there must have been at least 250,000 lambs slain, yet God says kill *it*, and when I see *the blood* I will pass over you. This month was unto them the beginning of months. And so when you, my dear friends, become sheltered under the blood, this month shall be unto you the beginning of months; your past history is, as it were, blotted out, and you become new creatures in Christ Jesus. You were dead in trespasses and in sins; but the moment you touch the blood, the "precious blood," that moment you are saved, every sin becomes blotted out, and this gives you a new existence; yours is a new life, even the beginning of months. The household may be too little for the lamb, but the lamb never too little for the household.

It was not their understanding the *theology* of the blood that saved them; it was their doing what God told them to do. "Believe on the Lord Jesus Christ, and thou shalt be saved." Men now-a-days teach and preach about Christ in His manhood character as the great exemplar, and extol Him as a moral teacher. But beware! it is the blood alone that can make atonement for the soul, and "without the shedding of blood is no remission." Will you trust the precious blood? If you trust it not, you trample it under foot, and reject it, counting it an unholy thing. Mark you, dear friends, God never intended the blood of the slain lamb to be trampled upon. The blood was not to be

sprinkled upon the door-step, but upon the lintel and the
two side-posts. Further, the lamb was to be roasted with
fire, and eaten that night. The sprinkled blood saved Israel
from the destroying angel, but it did not give them strength
and sustenance. It is one thing to have Christ as our
Saviour, but quite another to take Him as our life and
strength. Oh, if Christians would read their Bibles as
much and as diligently as they do the daily papers, there
would be no need for ambulance waggons to help on a weak
and hungry church ! There is no food for the quickened
soul apart from the book which tells of the Lord of life
and glory. Christians, read your Bibles, and feed upon the
Lamb—the Lamb slain from before the foundation of the
world.

The speaker continued to dwell upon the way in which
Jesus is inviting sinners to Himself, beseeching them to be
reconciled to God, and in deep earnestness of spirit pleaded
with the anxious ones to trust the precious blood of the
Lord Jesus Christ. In conclusion he said :—

Why doubt God ? He says that the moment you believe
in the precious blood of Christ you are forgiven, and have
everlasting life. ' The poor sinner is not only pardoned,
but justified from the debt of sin ; because the debt has
been paid by another — even the Lord Jesus Christ.
Eighteen hundred years ago He paid it all ; He loved me and
gave Himself for me. You have not to make your peace
with God ; Jesus made it for you ; He hath made peace by
the blood of His Cross.

Thus through the blood of Jesus I have redemption,
pardon, forgiveness, peace, sanctification, cleansing, victory,
home—sweet home ! all through the precious, precious
blood !

Who to-night will reject the blood ? Who will despise
the blood ? Who will leave this church to-night without

trusting the blood of Jesus Christ? Mighty God! bless this simple word of Thine to these dear friends. It may be the last time I shall ever speak to you, dear American people. Since I came among you I have received nothing but love and kindness, and I want you just now to trust the precious love of Jesus, and know your sins forgiven. God bless you, my dear, dear friends, for Jesus' sake. Amen.

Dr. Hepworth, on the part of the congregation, affectionately bade Mr. Moorhouse farewell, and after the benediction was pronounced by Dr. Dowling, many lingered behind to shake his hand and say good-bye.

A writer in the *New York Evangelist* describes his work in Rochester, Mass. :—

"We have recently had the pleasure of hearing in Rochester the English evangelist and Bible-reader, Henry Moorhouse. He spent two weeks in that city, holding daily and nightly services, and in spite of the intense cold of that month—the thermometer often standing from ten to fifteen degrees below zero—people flocked to hear him. Those services had so won all hearts to him, that the warmest of welcomes awaited his second visit, and we count it the richest spiritual blessing of our lives to have heard him.

"Youthful, almost to boyishness, in figure and appearance, you wonder at first where lies the spell that draws people so irresistibly ; but one look into those clear grey eyes reveals such earnestness, sincerity, and perfect transparency of soul, you trust him without an instant's questioning. His whole face wears the calm, untroubled look of a soul at perfect rest in God. His voice is clear and winning ; his delivery rapid, especially in his readings, as if the time were all too short for what he has to say. And all too short it is for those who hang with breathless interest on his words. Everything in manner and matter is the farthest possible remove from anything like sensational preaching. Utterly without self-seeking, the one aim and desire of his life is to lead sinners to Christ and Christians to a life of truer consecration to Him. A full and free salvation he preaches, and preaches with all the earnestness of his soul, but not a salvation that involves no Christian living. In this he is emphatic.

" His readings are marvellous. His unbounded love and reverence for the Bible and its constant study have given him a deep insight into its very heart; and the freshness, beauty, and originality of thought in these readings are a constant surprise, sometimes making every verse of a Psalm, that from childhood has been familiar as the alphabet, a new illuminated text.

" The flashes of genius all through his readings and sermons ; the wonderful aptness of his illustrations, driving the truth home irresistibly, and linking both truth and illustration so perfectly that one can never be recalled without the other ; his astonishing memory, that carries a score of texts at, perhaps, a single reading, scattered from Genesis to Revelation, naming book, chapter, and verse that the congregation may follow him in their own Bibles, with not a bit of paper to aid his memory, and never an instant's hesitation in recalling a text or expressing a thought of his own—these all gave him great power over an audience.

" His intense love for souls and his boundless love for the Master are the key-notes of his life; and the tender, beseeching earnestness with which he strives to win even the most fallen and depraved to Him, and the startling power with which he speaks to the consciences of those who have already named the name of Christ, will never be forgotten by those who heard him.

" The last service on Sunday evening drew by far the largest congregation ever gathered within the walls of the brick church. Before seven o'clock the entire audience-room was filled, the galleries crowded to their utmost capacity, the aisles below filled, and every inch of standing-room taken. The stair-ways and lecture-room were also filled with people, glad to stand within sound of his voice, though they could not get a glimpse of his face, while hundreds went away who could not gain entrance anywhere.

"Mr. Moorhouse has carried with him to his English home the loving gratitude of thousands of Christian hearts who have been made better for a lifetime by his visit; and when he crosses that wider sea, he will find hundreds, we doubt not, brought there by God's blessing on his earnest labours, waiting to welcome him into the joy of their Lord."

CHAPTER VII.

Bible Teaching.

" Preach the Word."—2 TIM. IV. 2.

LAY-PREACHING, so called, is a marked feature of the evangelism of our time. So indeed it has been in every period of a revived or a reviving Christianity. It is simply the witness-bearing to Christ of men taught by His Spirit, men who speak only because they believe. This kind of preaching has a charm of its own. Its flavour is the flavour of nature, rather than of art. Its fragrance is the fragrance of the wild flower, rather than of the garden plant. It is the utterance not of the professional or trained advocate, but of the witness who can bear testimony to the facts.

Wherein lies the charm of good lay-preaching? It is natural speech, strong and incisive, unaffected, unclerical, without smell of the midnight lamp, without starch of system ; not mathematically square or theologically exhaustive ; a witness-bearing rather than a sermonizing, a heart utterance more than a head exercise, language with hands and feet, that is to say, words in which the truth, fitly embodied and alive, walks up to the very faces of men, and with outstretched hands takes hold of them in loving violence ; speech full of the light of eternity, and the solemnity of coming judgment, yet never harsh but always well moistened with tenderness and love, regard for the opinions and likings of mortals being utterly swallowed up in the one great aim to glorify God in the salvation of sinners. True lay-preaching was born at Pentecost. Its tongue of fire is fed, not with any fine gases of rhetoric, scholasticism, or philosophy, but with oil direct from the Golden Bowl. Out of its native Pentecostal element, it speedily languishes, and becoming corrupt it develops into all manner of unpleasant vapours, into self-inflations and self-advertisements, and the magnifying of its apostleship above all apostleship. When once a lay-preacher goes self-ballooning, you may see him again in the flesh, nay you will likely see him too much in the flesh, but you will not see him in the Spirit any more.

Owing to the lack of a body of doctrine in the preacher himself, or the want of that sobriety of mind that is begotten by a long and hard course of study, or from deficiency in grace or common-sense, lay-preaching is apt to degenerate, and so become weak. And weak it sadly is, when it goes to noise, or rant, or rhapsody, or childishness, or a mere text-string, or a beginning at Genesis with intent to do the entire canon, the high vulgarity of cant or the low vulgarity of slang, or anecdotism, or a kind of light, jaunty, jolly air not unsuitable to the selling of knives and razors, needles and tape, or the same speech over and over, and over again, till the spirit of the thing has fled, and the preacher carries about the dead body of a once living address, as the showman carries about his Egyptian mummy for exhibition.

Not such was Henry Moorhouse. He had in him the true fire, and he kept it burning. His fire was bright and steady, not glaring and fitful; so did he feed it with the truth. At an early stage of his course he found the Word of God as few believers find it, and he learned to use it as few evangelists can. This was the mainspring of his power, his admirable characteristic as a servant of Jesus Christ.

When the great Augustine was in the midst of his soul's crisis he went into the garden one night with his friend, also an inquirer, to seek retirement and converse. Leaving his companion in a little bower, he sought for a place where he might enjoy solitude and secret prayer, for his heart was bursting with the inarticulate cry, " Lord, what wilt Thou have me to do?" But here he could not pray, being disturbed by the sound of a voice issuing from a neighbouring house. He was constrained to listen. It was a child singing, and there fell strangely upon his ear the curious refrain, " Take and read ! take and read !" It was the voice of God answering his prayer ere yet the unutterable groanings of his heart had found expression. Hastily bending his steps back, he said to his friend, " Give me the Book." The Bible was opened, and the portion on which his eye lighted was Rom. xiii. 11—14, " And that, knowing the time, that now it is high time to awake out of sleep : for now is our salvation nearer than when we believed. The night is far spent, the day is at hand : let us therefore cast off the works of darkness, and let us put on the armour of light. Let us walk honestly, as in the day ; not in rioting and drunkenness, not in chambering and wantonness, not in strife and envying. But put ye on the Lord Jesus Christ, and make not provision for the flesh, to fulfil the lusts thereof." He read and bowed his whole man as before the majesty and at the burning feet of the glorified Redeemer. Then and there he entered into covenant with his Lord, whose most free and sovereign grace he henceforth lived to extol, and publish in a testimony that has outlived many centuries and instructed many generations.

At the beginning of his public career Henry Moorhouse

seemed to hear a voice from heaven, saying, "Take up and read! Take up and read!" He took up and read, as few Christian teachers read, the Word of God. He was pre-eminently the man of one book. Uninspired writings he did not despise; but, what to him was the rushlight in presence of the sun! It is told of the godly young English king, Edward VI., that once, in a meeting of the Privy Council, when one of his ministers stepped upon a large Bible in order to reach a high shelf, the pious monarch rose from his seat and, reverently lifting the Book of God with both hands, kissed it, and pressed it lovingly to his bosom : an act worthy of a king. Henry Moorhouse, perceiving that the Word of God is slighted even by its friends, raised it from the dust, where too many English Christians have been willing to let it lie, and pressed it with life-long reverence and love to his heart. Henceforth neither prayer-book nor hymn-book, neither confession nor catechism, neither commentary nor treatise, nor anything else of literary kind, was permitted to interfere with his incessant, intense, prayerful study of the Scriptures. He had heard the voice of the Eternal, and so full and clear did the voice fall on his ear that he almost became deaf to its human echoes. Thus he became more than an evangelist : he became a teacher of the disciples, a pastor of the flock of Christ.

In his study and exposition of Scripture Moorhouse had fallen on a method very much his own. His way was to search the entire Book of God for all the passages bearing on some given truth or theme. These texts he would arrange sometimes in the order of revelation in time, beginning with the first gleam of light and following it on to the high noon of full New Testament day. For instance, in his famous and powerful lecture on Atonement by the Blood, in which he has been successfully followed by several of our best evangelists both in this country and in

America, he starts with the first shadowy, but undoubted reference, to this fundamental doctrine of the gospel in Genesis, and pursues the " scarlet thread " throughout the Scriptures until the triumphant songs on the blood of the Lamb, as sung by the Church in glory, are reached in the Apocalypse. Sometimes, however, he pursued his theme in the order of systematic doctrine, dipping here and there into the Word and bringing forward the text passages in the logical or experimental order of the various parts or aspects of the truth under consideration.

It may interest the reader to know how Moorhouse fell upon this method of searching and handling the Scriptures. On one occasion, when about to address a public meeting of professing Christians, he found himself without a discourse and without time to prepare one. He had exhausted his addresses in the sermon style, he felt he had reached the end not only of his anecdotes and other illustrations but also of matter suitable for a regular discourse. His only resource was prayer for direction and help. In his distress his eye happened to light on an almanac, and he noticed the subject for a particular month, Justification by Faith, was followed throughout the thirty-one days in a series of Scripture proofs. He saw at a glance his opportunity, and tearing out the leaf, took it with him to the meeting, though not without considerable doubt and fear. At the outset of the service he announced he would not preach a sermon, but instead would direct the attention of the audience to several portions of Scripture bearing on the vital theme of " Justification." Passage after passage was examined, the meaning of each given in a few pregnant words, with some homely but fresh illustration. The attention of the people in the subject was aroused ; the utterances of the Spirit were followed with absorbing interest and avidity. To the surprise of Moorhouse the experiment proved a perfect

success.   Charmed, informed, refreshed, the audience at
the close of the meeting expressed an earnest desire for a
repetition of the exercise.   This he fell in with, and from
that time, partly dropping the ordinary style of sermonizing,
he pursued and perfected this method, not without much
advantage to himself and blessing to many.

Of his method of studying and elucidating a Scripture
topic one or two specimens from a heap of rude outlines
may be given here.

I.—GOD'S LOVE.

Prov. xv. 17	Dinner of herbs.
Cant. ii. 4	Banner, Love.
Cant. viii. 6, 7	Strong as death.
Jer. xxxi. 3	Everlasting love.
Hos. iii. 1	Drawn by love.
John xv. 13	Greater love.
Rom. viii. 35	Who shall separate ?
2 Cor. v. 14.	Constraining love.
Eph. iii. 19	Passeth knowledge.
1 John iii. 1	Behold the love !
1 John iv. 8	God is love.
1 John iv. 9	Manifested.
Deut. vii. 7	Why He loves.
Zeph. iii. 17	He will rest.
Rom. v. 8	God commendeth.
Isa. xxxviii. 17	Delivered me from pit.
Eph. v. 2	Gave Himself.
Rev. iii. 19	Loves and chastens.
John xiii. 1	To the end.
Gal. ii. 20	Personal.
Rev. i. 5	Loved and washed.
Isa. lxiii. 9	He redeemed.
Rom. viii. 37	More than conquerors.

II.—OUR LOVE.

John xxi. 15—17	....	Lovest thou Me?
Ezek. xxxiii. 31	....	Mouth love.
Matt. xxiv. 12	....	Wax cold.
John xvii. 26	....	His love in us.
2 Cor. viii. 8	....	Show proof.
Phil. i. 9	....	Love abound.
1 Thess. i. 3	....	Labours of love.
1 Thess. iv. 9	....	Brotherly love.
Heb. x. 24	....	Provoke to love.
John iv. 42	....	We believe.
1 John iii. 17	....	How dwelleth?
1 John v. 3	....	We keep His commandments.
Deut. xiii. 3	....	To know whether we love.
Deut. xxx. 16	....	Commanded to love.
Deut. xxx. 20	....	Life, love, obedience.
Psalm v. 11	....	Love and be joyful.
Psalm xxxi. 23	....	He preserveth.
Psalm xcvii. 10	....	Love—and hate evil.
Luke vii. 42	....	Forgiveness and love.
John xiv. 21	....	Love, and keep His commandments.
Rom. viii. 28	....	All things work together.
1 Cor. ii. 9	....	Things prepared for them.
1 Cor. viii. 3	....	He knows them that love.
Eph. vi. 24	....	Grace be with them.
1 Thess. iv. 9	....	Taught of God.
1 Pet. i. 8	....	Not seen, but love.
1 John iv. 19	....	Love Him because He.
Psalm cxvi. 1	....	Because He hath heard.
1 Cor. xvi. 22	....	Be accursed.

Such outlines seem to be sufficiently bare; but as

handled by Moorhouse there was no tediousness, no dry-
ness, no lack of interest, warmth, or power. In this way
he taught his hearers to reverence the pure, unmixed
utterances of the Holy Spirit. The Bible to too many is
much like any other book. This feeling of irreverent
familiarity with it is the bane or the loss of many a reader.
It was a lesson to notice his regard for every little word,
every jot and tittle of the sacred volume. For instance, if
one in quoting John iii. 16 gave the passage, as "God so
loved the world," he would invariably point out the omission
of the introductory word "for." See how that little word
links this glorious text with what goes before, and read,
"For God so loved the world." His extreme, but not
superstitious, reverence for the Book was singular. He
would not suffer anything, not even a sheet of paper, to be
laid upon his Bible. There alone, apart, it must lie, unique,
matchless, wonderful, the very mind and presence of the
infinite and eternal God.

Effectively as Moorhouse could preach in the ordinary
evangelistic style, his chief excellency and power as a
teacher lay in his Bible expositions. He could make the
Word itself speak. This is, perhaps, the highest function of
the Christian teacher, the perfection of his art. In his
expositions of an entire book of Scripture, his interpretations
were sometimes fanciful, and his lessons far-fetched; but
even in his conceits and fancies he did not go further afield
than good old Matthew Henry, while his deductions were
often as skilfully drawn, and as quaintly expressed as any of
that famous commentator's. His lectures and readings
were often suggestive, and sometimes original; and able
pastors were not ashamed to acknowledge that under his
humble leading they had got upon a fresh line of thought.

At his Bible-readings could be seen ministers, physicians,
lawyers, and other professional men, persons of education

and refinement, accustomed from one Lord's-day to another
to listen to the most elaborate discussions of revealed truth ;
Christian workers of every class ; with a crowd of the
common church-going people ; all deeply interested in the
lessons of spiritual wisdom drawn from the Word of God,
by this ingenious but unsophisticated commentator.   There
must have been power somewhere ; in what did the secret of
it lie ?   First of all, no doubt, it was the Holy Spirit in the
teacher, and in His own truth thus honoured.   Subsidiary
to this, his power lay partly in his quick and fine perception
of analogies betwixt the natural and historical on the one
hand, and the spiritual and experimental on the other ;
partly, too, in his large and firm grasp of vital truths and
principles, and his power of setting them forth in all the
glowing colours of lively fancy and fervid emotion ; but chiefly
in his holy sympathy with the mind of the Spirit, which he had
attained by the labour of many years in the loving and
prayerful study of the Scripture.

One of his favourite books for public reading and
comment was the profoundly interesting and exquisitely
beautiful story of Ruth.   The parallel between the history
of Ruth, and the no less picturesque story of a soul's return
to God, or the espousals of the Church, the bride of the
Lamb, is easily enough drawn ; and it is too easily over-
drawn.   But only a shallow reader or an unreasonably
matter of-fact literalist will deny that in such a narrative it
is hardly possible to avoid touching great principles, striking
universal chords, and gathering practical lessons.

Naomi and her husband repairing to the land of Moab
under the pressure of famine, supplies our preacher with
a suitable text for illustrating the folly of God's people in
going down to the world for comfort and help.

The afflictions of the Israelitish matron in the heathen
land of her sojourn afford him an opportunity for warning

Christians of the sorrows that wait upon any compromise with the flesh or unwarranted fellowship with the world. The return of Naomi to the land of her fathers is the canvas on which our preacher depicts with graphic strokes the wandering soul returning to the Lord. In the two young widows he sees the two great typical classes of inquirers. With close, heart-searching application and tender pathos he describes the parting of the ways, where Ruth finally strikes for the land of Israel and the God of salvation, while her half-enlightened sister-in-law decides for the old heathenism and takes her melancholy way back to idolatry and death. Then the picture brightens. Ruth is gleaning on the field of Boaz, finds favour with the rich and pious farmer of Bethlehem, and at the close of the day bears home her precious burden of the staff of life. Here the preacher's fancy takes wing, and little touches of humour serve to carry the lessons home. Ruth gleaning on the field of Boaz is the hearer of the Word. One typical hearer carries away from the field in a mass both grain and straw ; a needless labour, since a little discrimination might have effected on the spot a separation of the useful grain from the unprofitable straw. Another hearer, type also of a class, leaving the good grain of truth and wisdom behind, carries away in his foolish memory only the straws of oddities, absurdities, or trivial remarks, to be found in too great abundance on many a field. Happy the hearer of the gospel who, Ruth-like, has learned not only to glean but to thresh, and to bear from the field of divine ordinances the full measure of pure grain.

In his Bible-readings he was wont to enlarge on the necessity and importance of the Christian's separation from the world. Grace, in his view, was no more grace, if it blossomed not into holiness. The innate and well-nigh irradicable Antinomianism of the human heart renders this teaching always seasonable. To some who claim to be disciples of Christ, said our preacher, the ancient triple enemy, the devil, the world, and the flesh would seem to have abandoned the field, and to such, therefore, there is neither foe nor fight. To others, who believe the flesh to be a source of some danger, the great adversary is only an abstraction ; and nobody is fool enough to fight with an abstraction, the mere shadow of an ancient superstition. As for the world, it seemed to our evangelist, as if the greater number of Christians no longer regarded it as hurtful to the soul or hostile to God and His Christ. Who that looks around on the churches and on Christians in social life with a spiritual eye will deny that his jealousy was a wise and a holy jealousy, and that his teaching on this head was in good season? In his warnings against its carnal maxims, its seductive friendships, its unholy pleasures, and, most of all, its lying religion, he was wont to wax indignant and to pour out his most scathing rebukes. He drew a picture of ancient Israel, from the shores of the wilderness, where they stood a newly-ransomed people, sending a duly chartered vessel across the Red Sea to fetch flesh and onions and garlic from the land of Egypt. Then another great ship is sent, and still another, until, at length, the great merchant fleet of the famous Flesh and Garlic line is established, with the colours of Israel and Egypt to be hung out on either shore ; and what with the new freedom and the abundance of Egyptian good things combined, the Land of Promise is lost to view or has faded into infinite distance. " What ! " he might well exclaim with mingled surprise and sorrow, " shall the newly-returned prodigal son, happy in his father's love, rise from the festive board, and, rushing into the dark night, make anew for the swine troughs, dragging the best robe in the mire ? "

" Should a Christian go to dancing-parties ? " was one

7

day asked by a young convert. "What do you think?" said our evangelist. "Suppose a young lady is affianced to a truly noble and good man, whom she tenderly loves, and there comes in a dastardly ruffian, who murders the bridegroom in the very presence of the bride. Now, if the murderer were to invite the bride to dance with him on the floor crimsoned with the blood of her beloved, tell me, should she consent?"

"Once I was commissioned by my brother," he went on to say, "to fetch from town a little article in gold which he wished to purchase. This I put into my pocket, where, from lapse of memory, it lay for several days in too close proximity to some leads I happened to carry with me. On recollection I drew the gold from my pocket, and, to my amazement and chagrin, found it had taken on the dull hue of its meaner companions. The lead had borrowed nothing from the gold; its complexion was as grey and coarse as ever; but the gold had lost its beauty, it had grown like its company, it was become dim. So, the world gains nothing from the worldly Christian, whilst, in his unwarrantable fellowship with the world, the Christian loses all his brightness and not a little of his worth. This illustration made a deep impression on the minds of many who heard it; and in one instance the impression took shape in the following lines:—

> "I had once a precious trinket
> For my watch—a golden chain;
> How it glittered in the sunshine,
> Thus reflecting light again!

> "But my golden chain was carried
> Where a leaden plaything lay,
> And a few short hours of friction
> Wore its brightness all away.

" While the plaything was not brightened
  As it lay against the chain,
Whence it stole all-glorious beauty—
  (Will it ever shine again ?)

" Now the light no more reflected,
  Every link seems dark and cold,
As a trinket now rejected,
  I can scarce believe it gold ! "

To speak and act like the world is only too easy for the Christian to learn. To make the lesson pointed and memorable he was wont to tell of a canary which, placed in the same cage with a sparrow, lost its own sweet song and learned to chirp like its vulgar and unmusical companion. This illustration also found its way into verses, evidently composed by the same hand :—

" O my birdie !—like a fairy
  With your soft and lightsome wing,
O my golden sweet canary,
  How I loved to hear you sing.

" But you listened to a sparrow
  With his shrill, discordant tone,
And, my beautiful canary !
  All your melody is gone.

" Like a sparrow you sit chirping,
  While he's never learned your song ;
He has still his feeble twitter,
  Chirping, chirping all day long.

" You have taught me a sad lesson,
  Fraught with deep and solemn pain,
That if I with sinners mingle
  I shall lose, and they—not gain."

Thus in his own homely way he taught great lessons in little parables. He loved much to enlarge on the grace of God, so rich and free in Christ our Lord. " Grace " he was wont to say, " is—

The Bread of Life seeking the hungry.
The Living Water seeking the thirsty.
The Garments of Salvation seeking the naked.
The Truth seeking the liar.
The Rest seeking the weary.
The Light seeking the darkness.
The Pardon seeking the guilty.
Mercy seeking the wretched.
Life seeking death.

" Grace is all this in the person of our Lord Jesus Christ seeking and saving that which was lost."

Simple are such teachings ; and yet they are remembered by the common people, aye and by the educated, when profounder discourses are forgotten.

His power of apt illustration always served him well. Addressing the Christian people of Dundee he read, from Acts xxviii. 1—6, the story of the viper fastening on the hand of Paul. "What hinders the gospel in Dundee ? What causes the world to stumble at the truth ? " he boldly asked ; and as boldly answering his own question he said, " It is *the viper of inconsistency* that has fastened on your hearts, and is thus leading unbelievers to a conclusion as melancholy as the belief of the barbarians who supposed Paul was a murderer. Shake off the viper ; be out and out what you profess, and the people of the world around you, like the savage islanders when they saw the venomous beast drop into the fire, *will change their mind.*" Some, in the audience that evening, frankly confess they were then smitten with a sense of their inconsistency as Christians ; and they gratefully acknowledge their elevation to a happier and worthier spiritual state through the instrumentality of Henry Moorhouse.

At our Noon Prayer-meeting he was one day reading in Luke, fifth chapter. Pausing at the words, " but the fishermen were gone out of them (the ships) and were washing their nets," he glanced from the page to the audience, and observed quaintly, " The Lord will not use a dirty net." This simple remark proved to be as a nail fastened in a sure place.

" I don't have assurance," frankly said a Christian young man at a Bible reading in Dundee, when that somewhat vexed subject happened to come up. " What is your name, sir ? " inquired our evangelist. " J—— C——," was the reply. " How do you know ? " demanded Henry. " I have always borne that name," said the other. " But are you quite sure that is your name ? May there not be a mistake about it ? " " I am perfectly sure," was the answer ; " my father gave me that name, and as he happened to be Session Clerk (Parish Registrar), I have his own handwriting for it, and there can be no mistake." The quick-witted evangelist, seizing the last answer, immediately drew the attention of the young man to the Word, in which the Father has with His own hand engrossed a certification of name and sonship, such as may well satisfy every rightly-instructed, veritable child of God. This important point Moorhouse was able to set in a clear light, without confounding, as too many lay-evangelists do, assurance of personal salvation with faith. Wisely and tenderly did he deal with the timid or dejected believer, who doubts not his Lord but himself. *To believe in Christ* is one thing ; *to know* that *I* believe is another and a different thing. This distinction is too often overlooked.

Owing to the operation of a variety of causes, there are always some true believers who lack certitude as to their own interest in Christ. It may be deficiency in knowledge, or weakness of faith, or the prevalence of some subtle form of sin, or the sloth that gives not needful diligence to make the calling and election sure, or strong temptation from Satan, or the habit of introspection, or feebleness of mind, or melancholy, that "devil's bath," in the waters of which, as the old divines were wont to say, the great adversary of the soul disports and refreshes himself, or finally, for aught we can tell, the cause may lie in some inscrutable purpose of God, a region far too remote for human wisdom to investigate. Here lay-evangelists often fail. Because unconverted people are only too ready to take refuge in the lie, " Nobody can tell whether or not he is saved," or in the half-truth, " Every one hasn't assurance," evangelists in their eagerness to collar the sinner are apt to cuff the Christian, whose fear is greater than his joy, and his hard thoughts of himself a better evidence of grace than much that passes for assurance. In fact, we are not able, often, to argue a doubting soul into consciousness of personal salvation. Somehow, there are ever some who must grow into it. Much wisdom and tenderness is needed in dealing with such a case.

Mr. Moorhouse cultivated the fine art of illustration. Quick to discern analogies, he sought and found simile, metaphor, and parable everywhere. In one of his Bibles I count as many as five hundred headings of distinct illustrations. They are gathered from nature, from Scripture, from history sacred and profane, from biography, from science, from domestic life, and from every-day scenes in the world. Little children, flowers, animals wild and tame, ships, stars, kings, culprits, beggars, rich men, and a hundred other objects, are called in to do service in this connection. In short, his lively fancy seized on everything that his skill could make into a wrapper of spiritual truth-

Many of his illustrations were apt, not a few were striking, and some were not without poetic beauty. Here are two or three.

A little girl in the slums of London wins the prize for a flower growing out of an old, broken tea-pot; her success in training the plant being due to the pains she took in always placing her flower in the only corner of the window favoured with a sunbeam. A lesson for the Christian to walk in the light.

A rough, enraged at his dog for losing in a fight, cruelly throws it into the lion's cage in a menagerie : but the noble brute, instead of destroying the helpless incomer, which innocently walked up to his king and sat beside him, seemed to take pleasure in his new companion. Seeing this, the owner of the dog began to insist on the keeper fetching him out ; but the latter refused, saying that he who wanted him must fetch him out for himself. So the soul that seeks safety with the Lion of the tribe of Judah needs not fear Satan : let the adversary fetch him out if he can.

Standing at the window one wintry day, he sees a poor, ill-clad child taking shelter from a hailstorm, in the corner of the gate. A working-man, passing that way, catches a glimpse of the little one, hastily retraces his steps, lifts him in his arms, and turning his back to the blast, lovingly presses the stranger bairn to his bosom. When the fierce shower is over, he sets the child down and passes on. That night our evangelist related the incident, and then amidst the tears of his audience, pictured the Son of God giving His own back to the pitiless storm of Divine wrath, whilst He hides the helpless sinner in His bosom.

I was in Kerry a little while ago (he says in one of his lectures), and I went out into a field along with a gentle-man who had a great many sheep. By-and-by we came to a mother sheep, with three of the sweetest little lambs.

"Is not that a pretty sight?" I said. "Yes, but I am not going to let her keep them all : I am going to take one of them away." "What will the lamb do?" "I will give it to a goat to bring up." "Did you ever do that before?" "Yes; two years ago that same sheep had three lambs ; I gave one of them to a goat to bring up. By-and-by the lamb grew, and was able to eat grass ; then I took it away from the goat and put it among the sheep; but that lamb never heard the bleating of a goat, but it tried to get after it." What was the reason? It had been brought up on goat's milk, and had thus partaken of the nature of the goat. So it is with the sheep and lambs of Christ. We have been nursed on goat's milk, and when we hear the bleating of the goat, we want to go after it. But, thank God, we have a good Shepherd who knows how to take care of His sheep and lambs.

Even in his hasty, off-hand addresses, there was usually not a little good sense and point. Addressing the Flower Mission Band, Home of Industry, London, on 2 Kings iv. 8—37, "A great woman," he says :—

"1. This was a woman great for her *common-sense*, as seen in the simplicity of the nice little room she prepared for the prophet.

"2. She was also great in *contentment.* 'Wouldst thou be spoken for to the king?' She had no desire for introductions into society, or for luxurious living.

"3. She was great in the *care of her son.* Those who are simple in their households and of a contented spirit, are always careful of their children, and their husbands trust in them.

"4. She *went herself* to the prophet: this made her great. Why did she lay the boy on the prophet's bed, and not in the parlour or other room? The bed was the resting place of the prophet; so if he came while she was away, he would see her need. The prophet was in that what the Lord Jesus is to us. Oh, should we not bring our friends to Jesus?

" 5. As soon as she gets to the prophet, Gehazi came up to her. So it is with us. Ere we kneel long in prayer, some Gehazi comes to take our thoughts away from the Lord. But she seemed to say, I will neither trust Gehazi nor the prophet's staff. ' I will not leave thee,' she said, and in this she was great. So we can all be great. During this coming flower season, let us not put our trust in the flowers or the texts, nor trust in means or measures, but in the living God. All the means in the world will not give life to one soul."

To the poor widows he addressed a word of comfort from Isaiah xli. 10, " Fear thou not, for I am with thee ; be not dismayed, for I am thy God : I will strengthen thee ; yea, I will help thee ; yea, I will uphold thee with the right hand of my righteousness."

" You have been in trouble, and have gone to an earthly friend, and he said, Fear not, but did not give you a reason why you were not to fear. God gives us a reason and saith, ' I will strengthen thee.' The least thing He gives man to do, man needs God's strength. ' I am a coward,' you say. You tell the Lord that, and He says, ' I will help thee.' "

Speaking of working for Christ he says, " We all want power. Salvation is offered unconditionally, but for work afterwards there are conditions."

" It makes all the difference, if we are following religions, and not following Christ. The centre is the person of Christ."

" Elisha said he would not leave Elijah, while fifty sons of the prophets stood afar off. So it is to-day in London : where one man is following close upon the Master's footsteps, fifty are afar off."

" Elisha healed the spring, whereas these fifty sons of the prophets who had lived in Jericho for many years had not made a blade of grass to grow. Here is the man of God, the man of power, who by a single life-touch does more than all the fifty sons of the prophets had been able to do for years."

Speaking of God's love to men in the gift of His Son, he said, " *God gave the best thing in Heaven for the worst thing on earth.*"

While the chief note in the preaching of Henry Moorhouse was God's love to a perishing world, he knew well when and how to announce divine judgment and coming wrath. Like all other holy men from the beloved disciple downwards in every age, who drank most deeply of the love that passeth knowledge, he had the most awful sense of the holiness of God, and the future punishment of the sinner. His idea of God's love was not that of the mere sentimentalist or the purblind universalist. In fact, he published a tract in proof from Scripture of the eternity of future punishment. But while he taught the whole counsel of God, keeping nothing back, he exercised a wise discrimination as to the time and manner of setting forth a particular truth. Once, as he was going to preach to a set of notoriously wicked miners, one said to him, " Well, you ought to hold those men over the mouth of hell, and show them its horrors." " No," he replied, " I'll preach to them that God loves them, and sent His Son to die for them. But I'd hold over the mouth of hell some of those church members who care nothing for the love of Christ."

With some of his opinions many would not be able to agree. In the matter of Church Reformation his ideas were radical. He would not, perhaps, like some earnest men of our day, have pulled down the entire fabric, without furnishing any clear guarantee that the new building would

be marked by fewer flaws. But his ideal of church government and worship suffered from the infirmity of mere
theory. Besides, to model the government of the church
after the most perfect pattern, and to set up the purest form
of worship possible, does not necessarily secure the Christian
community against corruption, defection, and error. This
no government howsoever Scriptural, no creed howsoever
true, no discipline howsoever pure, can render permanent.
The Divine Head of the Church, and He only, by His Spirit
and sovereign working, can create and maintain life and
purity in the Church. In his later years Moorhouse came
to see this more and more, till at last nothing of the exclusive
spirit of the separatist seemed to remain in him. He did
not hate a man because he was the pastor of an imperfect
church. He would not excommunicate a minister because
he was ordained as an elder to teach and rule. He
embraced all who love the Lord Jesus. Only at the point
of fatal error he drew up. He would not worship or work in
a Unitarian place of meeting. " They deny my Lord," said
he ; " let them come to us, I cannot go to them." Nor
would he give countenance to men, however splendid their
eloquence or lofty their genius, if their teaching made void
the atoning sacrifice. Such preachers, he affirmed, at once
rob Christ of His glory and man of the only ground of hope
for eternity.

If he was extreme in some things, it is surely better to
sigh and cry because of abominations in the Church as well
as in the world, than to settle down in a time-serving accommodation to things as they are. His sense of the holiness
of God, and his vivid anticipation of the coming judgment,
when the wood, the hay, the stubble now piled on the " one
foundation " will be burnt up, filled the mind of Moorhouse
with a strong repugnance to everything false and unreal.
He longed for the time when there will be a kingdom of

God without one rebel in it, a Church of Christ without spot or wrinkle or any such thing.

His singular love for the Bible, more perhaps than the matter of his teaching, frequently made a deep impression on men of lofty character, communicating to their minds a new spiritual idea, or a fresh God-ward impulse. This was specially the case in America. " He brought us a new Bible, and almost a new Saviour," says the venerable Dr. Shaw, of Rochester, United States. " The Bible in his hands appeared to be a new revelation," writes Mr. Reynolds, of Peoria. " It was under God, through Henry Moorhouse," is the testimony of Rev. Joseph Kelly, Washington, " that this knowledge was brought to me, and so brought home as to change entirely the character of my work. The light poured in by him upon the pages of the Bible made it a new book. It was then seen to be a unit." " Christians of every name, and ministers with long years of successful work, and young converts entering the field, alike sat at his feet to study the Word," is the emphatic statement of his friend, Mr. D. L. Moody. " If Moorhouse had done no other work in America," says Mr. Needham in his " Recollections," "than that of bringing Mr. Moody and Mr. Kimber more directly into the heart of the Gospel, and in furnishing them with a key to its better understanding and its more vigorous proclamation, he would not have visited in vain, nor laboured in vain."

" Henry Moorhouse came to this city twice while he was preaching the Gospel in America," writes Rev. Dr. Brookes, of St. Louis, "and during both visits he was my most welcome guest. Thus it was my privilege to be brought into very intimate personal relations to him for a period of more than four weeks, and much of each day and night, when he was not engaged in public service, was passed in delightful conversation and prayer and fellowship in the truth. It was given me to see into his heart, and he drew forth my love with no ordinary fervour and tenderness.

"That which most impressed me in those pleasant days, the remembrance of which is still very sweet, was his singleness of purpose. He was a servant of one Master, a student of one Book, a man of one aim, a preacher of one theme. Nothing seemed to interest him apart from the Person, the Word, and the work of the Lord Jesus Christ; and, while playful as a child with the children of the household, he exhibited unmistakable signs of weariness, if visitors insisted on introducing topics of temporal and worldly character. It was amusing to watch his look of blank indifference when asked whether he had read some popular book, and listen to his quick reply, 'I have never heard of the book, and hope never to hear of it again.'"

But if a question were presented that touched the glory of the Lord, the honour of His word, or the welfare of the soul, he was on the alert in a moment. His eyes would open wide, and he was instantly ready with an answer taken from the Bible, which he usually had in his hand or near his side. He was evidently in full sympathy with the views of the late Duncan Matheson, who said in one of his last addresses, delivered at the Perth Conference, "I stand to-day with my eyes fixed on the *lost*. I plead with evangelists to keep at the one thing. With the vision cleared by heaven's lamp, they will see the crowd rushing on to destruction, sporting with death, indifferent to Calvary, laughing on the way to hell. . . . God, heaven, hell, salvation, are solemn realities. The shadows of eternity are falling on the path of some of us. They are not dark, but lightened by the glory that shines from the better land. I know not how it may be with me. Our Father can heal if He pleases. I leave it in His hands. It is sweet to know that we toil only a little while ; that, 'sowing in tears we shall reap in joy.' "

Indeed, he filled well the office of evangelist, and was a striking illustration of the truth that such an office exists, or at least ought to exist, as any intelligent person can see by reading Eph. iv. 11 ; Acts xxi. 8 ; 2 Tim. iv. 5. Dr. Eadie, one of the ablest and soundest commentators of the century, has well said upon the first of the passages here cited, " This official title implies something special in their function, inasmuch as they are distinguished also from teachers. These gospellers may have been auxiliaries of the apostles, not endowed as they were, but furnished with clear perceptions of saving truth, and possessed of wondrous power in recommending it to others. Inasmuch as they itinerated, they might thus differ from stationary preachers. Passing from place to place with the wondrous story of salvation and the cross, they pressed Christ on men's acceptance, their hands being freed all the while from matters of detail in reference to organization, ritual, and discipline."

If this language gives a true picture of the New Testament evangelist, it also presents an admirable portrait of Henry Moorhouse. He was furnished with clear perceptions of saving truth, and possessed of wondrous power in recommending it to others. It would be a great mistake to suppose that he was of dull intellect, for Jesus Christ, as the God of creation and providence, had conferred upon him a quick mind ; and his ' several ability' consisted of a substratum of good, hard common-sense, on which grace built beautifully. But, after all, it was Jesus Christ, as " the Author of eternal salvation," who made him what he was constraining him by His love, consecrating him, soul and body, to His service, filling him with intense and increasing desires to know moreand more of His Word, exalting that Word in the esteem of the uncultivated youth far above all the opinions and systems of all the schools and theologians, and thus putting into his hands weapons of warfare, by which, according to the fine rendering of Conybeare and Howson, he could " overthrow the reasonings of the disputer, and pull down the lofty bulwarks which raise themselves against the knowledge of God, and bring every rebellious thought into captivity and subjection of Christ." (2 Cor. x. 5.)

This independence and earnestness in the study of the Bible gave him great simplicity and boldness in preaching the Word. He was diligent and patient in his search for truth; but when it was revealed to him by the Holy Spirit in its radiant loveliness, he conferred not with flesh and blood, and never consulted consequences in his determination to exhibit it to others. The utter depravity of man's nature, even amid the appliances of human culture; the absolute necessity of the new birth by the Holy Spirit through faith in Christ as revealed in the Word; the atonement made by the blood shed upon the cross; the present and certain salvation of the believer; God's sovereign choice of His people; the wide-spread ruin that will be the end of the present age; and the personal return of the Lord Jesus as the hope set before the Church—were constantly proclaimed with remarkable clearness and force.

CHAPTER VIII.

𝕭ible 𝕾preading.

"But the Word of the Lord endureth for ever."—1 PET. I. 25.

DURING his latter years he went largely into the work of Bible-selling. This was no commercial speculation; nor was it even a mere scheme for the circulation of the Scriptures; it was a purely evangelistic work. By means of the Bible-carriage he simply and solely aimed to advance the kingdom of heaven, and to spread the knowledge of the King. Such was his faith in the Word of God, such his love for the oracle of saving truth, that no greater joy was his than the joy of putting this invaluable treasure into the hands of the poverty-stricken heathen of England, unless it were the supreme delight of winning a soul for Christ. He refused all remuneration by the sale of the book; any profits derived from the business were devoted to the purchase and gratuitous circulation of Gospel tracts and such like Christian literature. Every carriage was consecrated as solemnly as if it were a grand cathedral. Every movement was a missionary enterprise, every book sold was accompanied with invocation of the Holy Spirit; and every good day's work was celebrated with a renewal of the angels' song on the birth of our Saviour, "Glory to God in the highest; on earth peace; good-will to men."

To fairs and other places of public resort he took his

caravan, finding thus opportunities not only of putting the Word of God into the hands of vast numbers of the people, but also of preaching the Gospel to many thousands. The immediate results were frequently of a remarkable character ; hundreds were awakened to a sense of eternal verities, and many were converted. It was a work of faith, a labour of love ; but it could only have been carried on extensively and with success by a man possessed of a real talent for business. The old auctioneer was again at work; but this time it was not "Brummagem wares" of dubious value, but gems of purest gold and pearls of great price : and for foolish jocularities were substituted kind, gracious, holy words, with hearty benedictions on buyers and sales, and a joyful sounding of the jubilee trumpet amidst the din and hubbub of the world and its business. It is sad enough to know that England is so far a heathen country as to need Christian work of this kind, but it is, at the same time, gratifying to learn, as we do from the success of Henry Moorhouse on this field, that the heathenism of our land and day can be effectively assailed from many points, and that what the Church of Christ needs is not so much more bishops, as more Bible-carriages, and Bible-men, that is to say, men with the Bible in their hearts.

In March, 1878, he brought his large Bible-carriage to London, where, for a month, he resided with his fellow-worker in Christ, Miss Macpherson, the devoted friend and benefactress of the city arabs. The waters he had recently fished in had been fished out, as he said, and he was in search of fresh pools. Although in a state of extreme bodily weakness he gave a series of Bible lectures ; but his chief burden was the Bible-carriage, which was stationed at Whitechapel. Not far from "The Dublin Castle," could be seen in the evenings the two lamps of the carriage, flaring as brightly as any cheap jack's, while the evangelists and their helpers are busy selling the books and preaching the Gospel at the same time. One of the well-known ladies of the Home of Industry is leading "Hold the Fort" on a small harmonium ; her two sons are selling Testaments by scores ; some of the poor people are listening to the music and the hymn ; others are intent on making a purchase, and the great crowd is surging to and fro. Yonder is a poor man, standing and listening. Now and again he takes a shilling from his waistcoat pocket, and, after looking at it, replaces it. What is he going to do, he is asked by the lady at the harmonium, who notices his movements : will he buy one or two of the nice books? "Well," said he, " my missus gave me a shilling to-night when I gave her my week's wages, to buy myself a new meerschaum pipe, and this youngster wants me to buy him a book. Poor chap," he says, " he ain't got no dad ; so here goes. I'll have it all in books, and take my own chicks one apiece."

This poorly-clad working-man hands up his only shilling, and in return receives six twopenny Testaments. The quick eye of the miserable little arab boy begins to gleam ; and in another moment his face is mantled with smiles, and his heart chuckles with infinite delight as he presses to his bosom the coveted treasure, which comes to him as a wind-fall of rare fortune—a very God-send. The benefactor never imagines he has done anything worth talking about : and yet there is many a fine gentleman, and many a titled lady in the West-end, who spend their thousands on pleasures less ennobling and less satisfying than the joy that poor man finds as he hands the arab his little book, and carefully stows away in his coat pockets the remaining five for his own children. He probably never heard the Scripture saying, " It is more blessed to give than to receive," but all the same, he feels it in his heart, and this makes a world of difference betwixt one man and another. Pity the poor rich man who spends his all upon himself, and is not a whit the better for it, but the worse ; drop a tear for him as his carriage rolls past : but pull off your hat and bow to the noble and rich poor man who can sacrifice his last shilling and the new pipe in an act of genuine kindness and manly spirit. There is hope for England so long as this sort of man is found in the land.

All the while our evangelist is sitting at the end of the carriage platform, praying and coughing alternately. Too weak to address those crowds, he who had preached to thousands on two continents, is contented to be silent, but not to be idle. He sees the word of God having free course—passing into the hands of the poor—and he is happy. "Give the people the Word," he would say, " it will bring forth fruit : morning and evening sow the seed, it will not return void." Great was his joy when a noble-souled gentleman undertook to maintain a Bible-carriage for London. The opening day was to him a day of rejoicing and praise.

On one occasion he had dropped into a hall in London, where the Gospel was preached, but wrapped up in so much of human wisdom, that Henry's soul was vexed. "Come away," said he to his friend ; and on getting out, he stood and wept for a while in silence. "What is the matter?" inquired Miss Macpherson. "Oh, why will they murder the precious Gospel?" was his reply. "No heart, no tenderness, no love !" Then he brightened and added, "Get me the biggest hall in London, and every night for a month I will preach on 'For God so loved the world, that He gave His only-begotten Son.'" And weak though he was and burdened with the Bible-carriage work, he preached in various places, losing no opportunity of testifying with the living voice to the love of God in Christ Jesus our Lord.

In the following letters, although for the most part brief

and hurriedly written, we obtain clear glimpses of the man and his work :—

"STOCKTON-ON-TEES, *Feb.* 20, 1879.

"BELOVED MR. B.——, Your kind, loving letter made me very happy : 'tis so nice to hear one is not forgotten. But I was so sorry to hear your dear mother had gone home to her blessed Lord. How good the Lord has been to us since we all took tea together, several years ago ; dear Mr. Moody and your dear mother both being there. I told you then what a mighty man of God Moody was, but never dreamed he was going to be used so much as he has been. We are the same old friends we were then ; success has not made him proud. He uses his ten talents ; I use my one ; and we both together praise the Lord for using us at all. Dear Mr. Sankey is going to rest after next Tuesday. We go to Harrogate on Saturday ; then after I go to London for a month's special meetings, taking the Bible-carriage with me. It is doing a grand work, and does not hinder me in my own inside work, but rather helps. We can reach people now with the Gospel in the markets and fairs, who have never been reached before. And I could tell you of many now rejoicing in the Lord through this Bible ministry. I get the Bibles and Testaments from dear Mr. Müller, very cheap ; but the profits I spend in Gospel books, and give them away, so that I cannot be charged with making money out of the Bible. The cost per year will be about three hundred pounds ; but that is about one-tenth some societies spend in doing a great deal less work.

"Dear Lord C—— has gone home to rest. He is a very delicate gentleman. But I shall give him your kind invitation. He is one of the mightiest men in the knowledge of the Scriptures I ever met or heard, and as simple as a child. If you would like to invite him for meetings, you may mention me, and I am sure if the Lord leads him, he will come. His address is Earl of C——, Thomastown, County Kilkenny.

" My wife is very well. How often we have talked about you, and wondered how you all were ! Minnie, our daughter, cannot walk yet; but she is as bright as a bee, and as happy as a bird. We have a little son, seven months old, a sweet little fellow.

" We are having great crowds here : thousands come together, and many are blessed. Will you remember me to dear Mr. H——. With Christian love to beloved Mrs. B—— and your dear children. God bless you.

" H. MOORHOUSE."

" I thank you for your kind donation. My address will be until Tuesday, the Hon. Mrs. J——, Bolton House, Harrogate. Mrs. J—— is the daughter of Lord K——, and is a devoted Christian."

" *October* 1, 1879.

" I don't know how to thank you for your kind, loving letter ; 'tis long since I had such a one. Love seems in so many hearts to have gone to sleep. Some day it will awake again, and show its loving face once more. How true a good word maketh glad the sorrowful heart.

" I was five weeks in London. Dear Dr. Barnardo was worn out, and I went to take his place at the ' Edinburgh Castle.' We had most blessed meetings ; and about one hundred and fifty seemed anxious, and many, I trust, found a Saviour. I have often thought of the sweet hours I spent beneath your roof, and the true soul-fellowship I had with dear Mrs. —— and yourself. How glad I shall be to come again, I need not say : but it cannot be this month, as I am fixed for London, leaving on Friday (D.V.). I am so glad to be able to preach the glorious Gospel once more.

1 never thought I should, but the Lord has raised me up once more. My heart is very bad, and my cough as well; and I dread November with its fogs. Perhaps we could arrange a few meetings for that month at Chapel-le-Frith, or any of those places in which you take so much interest.

"Our little Minnie is a bright child, but cannot walk, paralysed since she was two years old; but she is a very happy little girl. Mary, my wife, joins in much love to dear Mrs. B—— and yourself. God bless you both!

"H. MOORHOUSE."

"EDINBURGH CASTLE, ST. PAUL'S ROAD,
BOW, LONDON, *Oct.* 25, 1879.

"BELOVED MR. B——, I could not tell you the joy to-day at the prospect, if the Lord tarry, of soon seeing you all once more. I would so much have liked to come to you during dear Mr. Haslam's visit. It does me good to meet him, and to hear him always helps me. He has always stood by me nobly at the meetings, and is a true man of God.

"I have been here for several weeks now, and have had crowded meetings of just the right kind of people. The hall seats over fifteen hundred. I have been no worse for the exertion; and such blessing as I have not seen since I was at Oldham last year with dear Lord C——! Over one hundred and fifty souls have confessed Christ as their Saviour, and some of them so bright. An old man, seventy-three years, as clear a case as one could wish. But 'tis so little amongst the masses! After all, I am convinced, after sixteen years of this work, that the only way to reach the masses, is to go to them in the streets, markets, and fairs. Where I reach ten in halls, rooms, and theatres, the dear brethren with the Bible-carriage reach a hundred in the markets, etc. And what is needed now is fifty Biblecaravans to go to every city, town and village, in dear old wicked England, and preach the gospel to the masses.

" D.V., we open a new Bible-carriage for London about the middle of November, and wish dear Mrs. B—— and yourself could be at the opening of it.

" What a fine Christian Captain M—— is. I give a Bible-reading on Monday next at Mildmay. He wants me very much to give the Conference Hall a month ; but I am afraid of promising as I did before and then had to break my promise.

" I hope you have had great blessing from the Mission. We never know when the fruit will appear, but it will if the true seed is sown. A man came up to me at Blackpool a few weeks since and told me he was saved sixteen years since through a text I quoted at the Promenade at South-port. Do you know Mr. M—— has given Mr. F—— notice to leave him next month ? I am so sorry, as he was reaching people in the factories that could not be reached in any other way. I am afraid our marvellous sale of New Testa-ments has had something to do with it. But 'tis a pity in these days of sin to neglect any channel of doing good for our blessed Lord. We shall not have much more time down here to do His work, and eternity with Himself will make up for every act of self-denial down here.

" H. MOORHOUSE."

The summer of 1880 found him in a hopelessly broken state of health, but full of his Bible-carriage work. Prayer for a carriage to move in Liverpool and neighbourhood begins to be answered, and he is full of hope and joy. " Don't trouble," he writes to a friend whose work for Christ is a little threatened ; " the Lord gave me this for you to-day, Psalm lvi. 9—13. Plenty of sail and a fair wind requires lots of ballast ; and, though the ship moves slower, it sails safer. So rest; don't fight them; the Lord will confound them, and you will praise Him soon. Had a grand Bible-reading on the 'Rock' last night . . . . . *Praise God for the 'Life of our Lord' for one penny.*"

"I saw the dear young sailor I told you about, so wonderfully converted through 'the Rest' at Highbury. He came here last week very bright and very happy. Worth all the money and labour dear loved Mr. Mathieson and others have spent on that place is that one bright case. I am feeling much better, thank the Lord, and hope to-morrow to be out among the crowds circulating the blessed Book."

In November he writes, "So glad you are back again to the old workshop, and hope you will have a blessed time this winter (if He tarries). I think the reason why goodness and mercy follow us is just because He wants our eyes fixed on the Object before us, which is the Lord Himself. The Shepherd's dogs are not to be compared to the Shepherd. I have been very unwell, and have had to give up regular work again. But I am feeling better again the last few days, and am thinking of coming to London this week about the London carriage. We have never had a donation towards its support, and several have promised; and I want your advice. Mr. Grove has all the management, and God has blessed it wonderfully. I think the sales have averaged over fifteen pounds a week since he took charge of it, and near—

TWENTY THOUSAND

copies of the Scriptures have been circulated from it. Other carriages all doing well, thank the Lord."

Whilst prayer was his constant, never-failing resort in connection with this work, he put every iron in the fire and wisely gave his attention to the most minute details of the business. For instance, he saw well to neatness and variety in binding, and endeavoured, as far as possible, to meet every taste ; and he was most successful in persuading others to sell or circulate the Book. His enthusiasm knew no bounds. "Take care! you have heart disease; you are a dying man," the doctors were constantly telling him. "Yes, I know," he would say, "but I desire to go home whilst preaching the blessed Gospel."

In two years, 1879 and 1880, no fewer than 120,000 Bibles and Testaments were sold, which, together with books and tracts given away, amount to some " 2,100,000 messages from Heaven to poor, guilty, and lost sinners." And yet these figures give only a faint conception of the entire work accomplished. The prayers, conversations, pointed words, addresses—in short, the living-voice work, with the spiritual results, it is impossible to tabulate. But that many were thus brought to the fountain of living waters, and many saved, and the way prepared for the spread of the Gospel among tens of thousands of the people, there is no room to doubt. And all this, with its eternal results, was, under God, accomplished by a man without money or health, by a dying man who had nothing left him but faith.

CHAPTER IX.

Last Days.

"Having a desire to depart, and to be with Christ; which is far better."—PHIL. I. 23.

HIS last year was one of much suffering. His cough grew worse. The enlargement of heart went on increasing, prostration from sheer weakness by day, and nights of anguish. Nevertheless calm, patient, indomitable, he held on his way, "faint, yet pursuing." He would die in harness; and this also was given him. His faith did not fail him; even at the worst he was cheery and hopeful. "What a friend we have in Jesus!" he would say. But a few weeks before his death he writes, "How wonderfully the Lord keeps providing for us day by day! I have realized more than ever the last two years what a loving God I have trusted. How I would like to see all your dear faces again, but I don't think I ever will *until He comes.* The doctors say my heart is twice the size it ought to be, and the least excitement may take me away at any moment. 'Tis all right: the Lord is my shepherd: goodness and mercy follow. We don't look behind at them: we look before us at the Lord. The shepherd's dogs are not the shepherd. I find it very sweet work to lean on the Rock, instead of talking about it; to look to the Lamb, instead of reading about Him; and to be taken up with the Master, instead of with the Master's work. ' Bless the Lord, O my soul, and forget not all His benefits ! ' "

The following letters afford glimpses of his last days.

"STRETFORD, MONDAY, *Nov.* 17*th*, 1879.

" BELOVED MR. B——, Your letter dated 14th, only received this morning : no use telegraphing, so write instead. I am able, thank God, to take as many meetings as you like. Just let dear Mrs. B—— and yourself do whatever you think is right. I shall be satisfied any way and at any place. Will come to you (D.V.) by evening train on Saturday next, arriving I think about 7.30. Going (D.V.) to London to-day to open New Carriage. Glorious time yesterday at Marple. A Model Hall : fifteen anxious souls ; praise the Lord ! God bless you both. In haste,   " H. MOORHOUSE."

" ROSE BANK COTTAGE, STRETFORD,
MANCHESTER, *Dec.* 8*th*, 1879.

" BELOVED MR. AND MRS. B——, Arrived safe home, found all well. My voice quite gone before six on Saturday. Can only speak in a whisper : now been in bed ever since. My cold is much better. Enjoyed my visit so much : it cheered me greatly, and I trust I left a blessing behind me. I am praying for Miss Alice to be made strong. Will write a long letter soon as I am able. God bless you all.
" H. MOORHOUSE.

" Kind regards to Mr. B—— and Mr. J——. Just as I had finished I received the enclosed, which, please, put in an envelope and send back when read. It looks bright for the French work."

" STRETFORD, *Dec.* 10*th*, 1879.

" BELOVED MR. B——, Thank you for your kind letter. I am glad to hear from the dear old place in which I have spent so many happy hours. The doctor says I shall have to stay in the house a month, perhaps all winter. My voice is gone, and if I shout the hardest, 'tis only a faint whisper. But all is well and peaceful. My heart can rejoice in Him, the blessed Lord, who never makes mistakes. And I know He is going to teach me something I never knew before. Will you thank dear Miss B—— for her kind letter: I will answer it some day. She likes letters, and she deserves one at least from me, she was so kind. Dear Miss Alice, tell her to trust and not fear. I send her Isaiah xli. 10. With love in the Lord, in which all here join, to beloved Mrs. B——, yourself, and all your household. God bless you all.

" H. MOORHOUSE."

"*Jan.* 3*rd*, 1880.

" Our new Bible-carriage will (D.V.) be ready very soon, and I hope to devote it chiefly to village work. That will be one for London, one for towns, one for villages. Then I have taken part of a shop on Ardwick Green, which will be opened on Monday week (D.V.) for a Bible and Tract Depôt, to sell Bibles very cheap. You would be glad to learn that we are meeting with great success among the Teachers with the Bible, as we planned at Ford Hall. But we are short of stock. We need about £150 worth for the Depôt and carriage.

" There is a little hitch in the French work. A gentleman has collected over £150 towards buying the publications, and I don't want to interfere with him.

" Looking forward to the spring for work in Derbyshire, and feeling much better. God bless you, beloved Mr. B—.

" H. MOORHOUSE."

" ROSEBANK COTTAGE, STRETFORD,
" *Feb.* 17, 1880.

" BELOVED MR. B——, Have been very ill since I left Ford Hall, but to-day am feeling much better. You will be glad to hear that the plans talked over with you about the Lord's work have prospered beyond all my expectations. Already we have sold over one thousand Teacher's Bibles, and the demand for them is just marvellous. Our new Tract Depôt, is doing well, and giving a testimony for our absent Lord day and night. The Bible-carriage is now at Oldham, and the Lord is sending crowds to listen to the Gospel. And the sales are wonderful; last week the best we ever had, taking over thirty-four pounds for the Scriptures alone. We hope to open our new Bible-carriage in a few days, and would much like you and your dear wife to be present at the opening. We will arrange it early in the afternoon, so that you won't be kept out in the night air. Mr. Cr—— and Mr. Ca—— have each given me fifty pounds for the carriage. I hope to work it myself, and expect our first trip will be Derbyshire. As we talked over last December, 'tis still on my heart to give three months to your county, and think April, May, and June would be the best time.

" H. Moorhouse."

" Dr. Gourlay's, Weston-super-Mare,
"*April* 12, 1880.

" Beloved Mr. B——, You will be sorry to hear that I have again to rest for three months. I could not tell you how disappointed I am. Came here hoping to get all right for a summer's work for the Lord, and now have to give it all up. Have held several meetings, and felt no worse for them; but the kind doctor I am staying with examined me, and then got in a London doctor (both Christians), and on Saturday gave me a thorough examination; the conclusion— nothing but rest and lying down, not even to take a walk for three long months, would do me any good. Heart very bad. But I can write to any of my friends, only I must lie down all the time. Will you ask the Lord to give me the needed patience. . . . . " H. Moorhouse."

"Stretford, *April* 22, 1880.

"Dear kind Friend,—My heart is very, very sad to-day. I left beloved Dr. Gourlay's house on Monday, and on Tuesday he was called home to be with his blessed Lord. I can hardly realize it to be true. He was so kind to me. Left four little children, and their mother died only eight months ago. I do indeed thank you for your loving invitation; and, please the Lord, I will come soon. I am trying to get the Lord's business settled up, so that without a care I can take the rest ordered by five doctors. 'Tis hard work to do nothing but lie down.

"Your heart will be rejoiced to hear of the continued wonderful success of the Bible-carriages. Last week the three carriages sold in the markets, etc., over sixty pounds' worth of the Scriptures. In Bradford alone, Brewster and Bartlett sold over one thousand five hundred New Testaments in three days. Manchester carriage doing grandly, going to the little villages and scattering the good seed.

"I hope dear Mrs. B—— likes the 'Beautiful Home.' Will gladly send her some for distribution, if she wishes it.

"H. Moorhouse."

He writes to the same friend of the continued success of the Bible-carriages, and looks forward to "a glorious summer's work among the neglected and poor." He "longs to be in the field again," and says he "would rather break stones and work for Christ, than have a thousand pounds a year to be idle." In July we find him in Dublin, at the Believers' Meeting; then in London, and thence home. His health somewhat improved, he plunges anew into work, and speaks of "glorious meetings," with anxious souls pressing into the kingdom. At Chinley, he, along with Lord C——, held special services, which were attended by crowds, and accompanied by much blessing from on high.

In one of his last letters he writes :—

"DEAR MISS B——, The Bibles are three shillings and elevenpence each ; so I owe you tenpence, which I enclose in stamps. Since writing last I have been very ill, and never left my room for a week, and don't know when I shall be able to get out again. But the Lord knows what is good for us, and never makes mistakes. I think of you all very often, and wonder if the cold has come to you yet. I am so glad to see the good news in the paper about Lady M——. God bless our Queen for remembering her in her sorrow. I am sure a blessing will come to dear Ford Hall for taking in the widow and the fatherless. I had a letter from Lord C—— yesterday. He says he has never been so well for a long time. I think Derbyshire air has set him up.

"I wonder how the new Coffee Rooms are doing. Will you tell your dear kind mother I am trying to get 'The Beautiful Home' brought out in a large-sized book, with a coloured cover, to sell for a penny to the poor, same size as is usually sold for sixpence. Our horse has gone lame, and I think will never be better—I mean the Bible-carriage horse. All at home are very well except me. I do hope you are stronger. With much love in the truth to your beloved father, and mother, and sister, and all the household. God bless you all !

" HENRY MOORHOUSE."

" Dec. 6, 1880.

" DEAR LOVED MR. B——, I really don't know how to thank you for your loving letter, and kind invitation to come to dear Ford Hall, which is very, very dear to me, having spent some of the happiest hours of my life there. But I cannot come yet. The doctor orders me south—to Bournemouth or to France. At present I am staying at home,

where I have every care that love can give me; but if the
Lord will, I hope to go south in January, should the
winter be severe; I think to Cannes. My Irish friends
have sent me a loving invitation to come and stay the
winter with them; if not, to Bournemouth. I am very
happy: not a care, not a trouble for either present or future;
all I leave to Him who died for me. Could I have a
trouble, 'tis for the past. How much harder would I work
for the Lord had I to begin again; but the past is blotted
out, at least my failures are. How good of you and dear
kind Mrs. B—— to shelter the dear lady and her family.
You have the thanks of thousands in England and Ireland,
I am sure. And I hope that now she will be as happy as
her Saviour can make her in her new resting-place. I
often pray for her, and shall continue to do so. I am so
ill. 'Tis near a month since I was out of doors, and my
nights are sometimes fearful. I hope to have the Bible-
carriage 'Reports' this week, and shall send one to you.
Enclosed tenpence in stamps, the amount over for bills sent
me by Miss Alice. With much Christian love to you all.
God bless you, beloved Mr. B——."

To Mr. and Mrs. C—— he writes :—

"Your kind letter came to me in the midst of great
weakness. I had a very bad night; several times seemed
as if I was suffocating from my heart; but the Lord brought
me through it all. How sorry we are to hear about your
suffering; but 'whom He loveth,' etc. I know He is taking
great pains with me; but I need it all. *I am nearly home
now*, and every care I have is cast on Him: my wife, my
chicks; His work entrusted to me—all are left with Him.
No one else is able to carry the burden for me; and He is
both able and willing. I suffer from heart disease and
bronchitis, and have never been outside for nearly six

weeks. 'Rest'—'rest' is the cry of the doctors ; and however much I wished to work now, I have not strength to do it. I am glad you have that dear saint near you (Mrs. H——). Will you please give her the enclosed 'Reports' : I only got them to-day. I think you will be pleased with the work. I know the Lord has blessed it very much. Twenty breaking bread at Darlington through the work. I could write you both such a lot, for I love you both dearly ; but Mary says I must stop, my breathing is getting so bad. So— with very much love from us both to you all, not forgetting Ann and Walter—God bless you all.

" H. MOORHOUSE."

To Major Whittle.

" 55, TIVERTON STREET, ARDWICK, MANCHESTER.

" DEAR LOVED BROTHER,—Just out of bed, first time for many a day. If I am not with the Lord, shall be real glad to see you next Tuesday. But I am very ill. Ask prayer for me to suffer for Christ better than ever I preached for Him. I only want to glorify Him. Let me know when to expect you. A cab from the station will bring you for two shillings, and we will have dinner or tea ready for you. With much love to dear Mr. and Mrs. M'Granahan. I am glad to hear of all the blessing : praise be to the Lord !

" H. MOORHOUSE."

After some eight weeks of severe illness, the end came. He was ready. He had committed wife, children, and work to Him whom he had steadily trusted and loved for twenty years. He had no care left. His Saviour, he had said once and again during his illness, was taking much pains with him. The furnace was hot, but he knew the Refiner was watching the crucible, and that he should come forth as gold. His sufferings were sometimes excruciating; but, said the strong believer, "the Lord makes no mistakes." He had worked hard for the Master, he had witnessed a good confession, he had fought a good fight; but now in the deep waters his supreme wish was to suffer better for Christ than ever he had preached for Him. " Do not fret," he would say, " it's all right ! it's all right ! "

On Sabbath, 26th December, he bade his wife and children good-bye. To his little girl he gave the text, " God is love," and to his wife he said, " He is love; I have proved it."

A friend entering the room inquired, " Are you trusting Him *yet ?* " Turning round he replied in measured tones, " Why do you say *yet ?* I have trusted Him for nearly twenty years, why should I doubt Him *now ?* I do trust Him." To his father, who was weeping, he said, " It's all right," and sought to comfort him.

A friend, coming in said, " Is it all right, my brother ? " To this he made reply, " Sure, sure, sure ; it's all sure and well." To another he said, " If it were the Lord's will to raise me up again, I should like to preach more on the text, 'God so loved the world.' " Willing to remain and work, ready to depart and rest, such was the prevailing frame of his spirit. His mind stayed on God, his was the " perfect peace."

Having bidden all around farewell, he seemed to pass away, but means employed by the physician had the effect of bringing back consciousness. It appeared as if he had returned from the region of perfected bliss. On opening his eyes he said to his wife, " Why have you brought me back to such dreadful suffering ? I was in heaven. Can you understand how I have been brought back from there ? " " No, I cannot," was her reply. " Neither can I," said he. Probably, he had been in one of those rapt states of communion with God in sleep, to which he was singularly habituated from his earliest Christian days. It is a fact that some believers, accustomed to seasons of no common fellowship with God, have in certain states been unable to determine whether they were asleep or awake, whether in the body or out of it.

He lingered on for twelve hours more ; and then, a little after twelve o'clock on Tuesday morning, 28th December, 1880, he passed into the presence of Him whom he loved, leaving behind a widow and two children to the care of Him who has said, " Leave thy fatherless children, I will preserve them alive ; and let thy widows trust in Me."

On the last day of the year, relatives and friends, a great crowd, gathered together, and, without hearse or coach, carried him to the last resting-place. Tearfully and lovingly his beloved brethren laid him in a Christian's grave, the cabinet where the Lord safely treasures the body of the saint, precious in His sight because redeemed by His blood, not less than the soul. After suitable addresses by esteemed brethren, the company, sorrowing yet rejoicing, for the light of the glorious hope of resurrection made their tears sparkle, joined in singing the hymns—

" I love to think of the heavenly land,"

and

" Shall we meet beyond the river ? "

That last day of 1880 was a chill winter day with much snow on the ground. It would naturally suggest to that Christian gathering the thought of an approaching New Year, when the chills and tears of this present troubled state shall disappear for ever in the presence of the glorified Redeemer come to claim the very dust that is His own. Then if a loving, lowly, Christ-like life is any evidence of saving grace, Henry Moorhouse will be found amongst those who shall "shine forth as the sun in the kingdom of their Father." "And so shall we ever be with the Lord." It was meet, therefore, that the band of devout mourners should conclude their touching services at the grave by singing—

> " Glory, honour, praise, and power,
> Be unto the Lamb for ever !
> Jesus Christ is our Redeemer,
> Hallelujah ! "

CHAPTER X.

Character.

"For he was a good man, and full of the Holy Ghost and of faith.
ACTS XI. 24.

MEN of influence are usually men of marked individuality. Of this there was much more in the character of the simple "boy-preacher" than was at first sight apparent. In his later years, especially, there was little angularity; his character was well-rounded; by means of habitual self-restraint the equilibrium of his spirit was well maintained, and in his most enthusiastic moments he exemplified "the meekness of wisdom." Yet, under the calm and child-like exterior there was a constantly-running spring of originality. He copied nobody; he thought for himself; he was himself in everything. This perfect naturalness lent a rare charm to his character, and a power which many felt, acknowledged, and enjoyed.

At the basis of his Christian character lay a decided, personal consecration, a most pronounced separation from the world. He believed he was forgiven much, and it was obvious to all, save himself, that he loved much. A joyful surrender of himself and his all to Christ was the permanent habit of his life. The cross came to him daily, as daily he came to the Cross. But he reckoned not that it came too often; he was happy, he was highly honoured in taking it up day by day, never dreaming of following the example of such as arrange for an occasional cross with long intervals of carnal ease between. What he had given to his Saviour he would not take back if he could. He had given himself to God. He kept himself for God, he found himself in God; this was the secret of his power.

Underneath the consecration of himself lay his strong faith. Strong it was in its simplicity and childlikeness. It was Christ, Christ in the Word, Christ always, Christ only. For his ministry he needed not the hundred and one helps without which most men dare not attempt to preach the Gospel. In his trust in the Word he was happy and strong. He did not think the Bible is behind the age; he knew full well the age is behind the Bible. His confidence in the sword of the Spirit was itself a sermon and a lesson to teachers and people. This was the blade with which the great Captain had cut off the head of the Goliath of hell; he was sure there was none like it, and his constant prayer was "Give it me!" It was curious, almost alarming, to see him stand up to speak amidst an assembly of learned divines and veteran Christians. In the council of war he was but a drummer-boy among generals and captains; yet somehow the beat of his drum touched the chord of sympathy, and he carried all with him.

To his faith he added courage. He was a Christian of the heroic stamp. In one of the last years of his life he requested his medical adviser to tell him the whole truth in regard to his physical condition; he was not afraid to learn he had soon to die. In reply the physician said plainly he could not live long—a certain affection in the region of the heart rendered a fatal issue only too certain, and if he continued to preach, the end would come all the more quickly. "How long do you think I may live if I desist from preaching?" inquired Henry. "Probably eighteen months," replied the doctor. "And how long if I continue to preach?" was the

next question. " Perhaps nine months," said the other.
"Very well," said our evangelist, in his quiet, happy way,
" I will take the nine months, and preach Christ as long as
I can." With this sword hanging over his head he continued
in the work, and the reader will not be surprised to learn
that for the rest of his time he preached with a power, a
mingled solemnity and sweetness unusual for him. Not
every servant of God would, in like circumstances, see his
way to pursue a similar course ; but, beyond question, that
calm, deliberate preference of the shorter period with the
preaching to the longer period in comparative silence was
a real instance of heroic faith and self-sacrifice. Deeds of
this stamp lift religion above the ordinary level and attest
its divinity and power.

The faith that refuses to believe in impossibilities is sure
to prevail. The evangelist of great power possesses the rare
gift of being able to create opportunities. Many good and
useful workers can labour only where a field is prepared to
their hand. Give them a church, a chapel, a meeting-house,
or some other convenient place for gathering the people ;
give them an audience ; give them all needful helps and
helpers in the work, and they will do the work, and do it
well. But without such things as go to make an opportunity, they are powerless. The greater evangelist is able,
when no such advantages exist, to call them into existence ;
to gather the people where they have never been gathered,
to arouse a slumbering community, to create the convenient
season, and thus bring matters to a solemn issue, simply in
virtue of the faith that can level the mountains. " Compel
them to come in," says the King. " If they would only
come in, I would do my part to serve them," says a loyal
but not heroic servant. But the servant of the loftier type
goes his way to the unwilling, and somehow succeeds in
compelling them to come in. The humbler order of

evangelist is the bird that can sing only in the sunshine. The evangelist of high degree, like the nightingale, gives his song out of season and in the dark ; he awakens sleeping men, and holds them awake by the spell of his soul-moving song. When on one occasion a country minister complained to Duncan Matheson that his field of service was too narrow, the Scottish evangelist inquired if he had gone round the parish and spoken to every inhabitant about his soul. "No," said the minister; "that would be of no use, for they would not receive me ; many of them would shut their doors upon me, if they knew my errand. What then can I do?" "If I were you," replied Matheson, "I would go round to every house in the parish, and if the doors were closed against me, I would cry in at every keyhole, "Prepare to meet thy God!" That is heroic faith. It is the will of God that this kind of worker shall succeed. Such a worker was Henry Moorhouse. Not poverty, not defective education, not the bitter remembrance of early follies, not opposition or scorn, not the coldness of friends, not bodily weakness and pain, with sleepless nights and wearisome days, not the solemn announcement of numbered months, not many things unpleasant to the flesh, stood effectually in his way : he believed on Him who sits upon the throne, and his was the courage to simply act upon his faith.

He was characterized by the warmth of his love for the brethren. There was a glow in his love; you felt its reality. At great evangelistic gatherings he could be seen busying himself in finding lodging for the strangers, in providing railway tickets and otherwise caring for their comfort, although this was probably much less his business than it was the business of others. A Christian acquaintance one day calling on him, intimated that he was preparing to go to America. Moorhouse discovering in the course of the conversation, that this man's resources were narrow, quietly slipped ten pounds into his hand, saying as they parted, "The journey is great, and it will not do to go without something in your pocket." He never could keep a shilling for himself when he saw a Christian brother or sister in want. In his simplicity he assumed that all other followers of Jesus would do just as himself did. Once a poor girl who had been converted under his ministry was in need of a dress. Henry took her to a Christian man who kept a draper's shop. "Here is a poor girl who wants a dress,' said he; "I daresay you could supply her from your shop." "With pleasure," said the other, and thereupon the young woman was invited to make her choice. Henry thinking he had sufficiently explained the matter, left the one Christian in the hands of the other. To Henry's surprise, next morning the bill was brought; and to himself fell the privilege, too rarely exercised by the children of God, of leaving a handful behind for the needy gleaner. "Business is business," the pious draper would no doubt say. True, but the too rigid practice of that maxim turns Charity to the door, and scarcely leaves Honesty behind the counter.

In the house of a pastor in America, noticing that the knives and forks were worn and broken, he resolved on replacing the faded articles with a new set on his return from England. The kind purpose was not forgotten. On his re-appearance at the house of the minister, he brought out of one of his portmanteaus a handsome set of the best ware he could find in England, his sole reward the joy of a loving bountiful heart. Nor was this a mere exception. It was his habit. Bibles and a large variety of useful things were laid up in store for every long journey, especially his American tours; and this giving away, this pleasing and making glad other hearts, he found to be not only a spring of pure happiness, but means of grace to himself and a real help in the work of Christ. Writing from America in the winter he says to his little daughter, Minnie, " Are you feeding the sparrows, Minnie ? Don't waste a crumb ; give them all to the little birdies." And yet, at that same time he was swimming in a sea of successful work. The love of souls did not lessen his sympathy with suffering creatures. Again and again he writes his Minnie thus, " It will soon be Christmas now ; be sure and put out the crumbs for the little birds."

He cultivated a holy, scrupulous tenderness of conscience. Much did he fear wrong-doing even in little things. Especially did he watch against the insidious influence of a mercenary spirit, or of any worldly motive in his work for God. To shut the mouth of the gainsayer, who is ever ready to charge the servant of Christ with sordid aims, he was accustomed joyfully to forego his just claims. He would accept no remuneration in selling the Scriptures. Once, when Bibles were to be supplied on more advantageous terms than the catalogue prices, in order to leave a fair margin of profit, he would not hear of the arrangement. He said he " should not feel happy in making gain out of the Word of God," and greatly preferred going on as before, selling the books at the price they cost him. Viewed from the commercial standpoint, this may have been a mistake ; but it revealed a noble spirit of self-sacrifice, and a high regard for even the faintest whispers of what he regarded as the voice of conscience and of duty.

One day, as he was walking with a friend, a waggon laden with hay, happened to pass. Engrossed with the conversation, Henry unthinkingly put out his hand, and drew a small handful of the hay from the cart. Suddenly, as if smitten by some painful reflection, he hurried after the waggon and thrust the few straws back into the mass. It is told of Cranmer, the great English martyr, that, deeply

grieved for his sin in recanting the faith, he held his hand
in the first flames of the fire that consumed him at the
stake, exclaiming, "This hand has sinned—this wicked
right hand!" A holy vengeance on himself is permitted
the Christian; and he may sometimes find it profitable to
restrain, even from what is lawful, the eye, the hand, the
foot, that had been wont to offend. Holiness in little things
is a higher attainment in grace than many imagine, and is
more difficult to reach than most suppose it is before they
try.

Moorhouse was a man of deep, genuine humility. His
chief ornament was "the ornament of a meek and quiet
spirit." In his later years, at least, he said nothing about
himself or his work. One might be long in his company
and never learn from his own lips that he had ever preached
a sermon or won a soul. He did not count his converts;
much less did he advertise to the world the round number
of them. He seemed to keep a watchful eye on the
approach of that most subtle of devils, spiritual pride.
"Down! down! down! Henry Moorhouse," was still his
deepest heart-utterance; "And up, up, up with my Lord
and Master Jesus!" Eliot, the famous missionary to the
American Indians, when no longer able to preach or visit,
was found reclining on his bed, in a state of complete prostration, but at the same time cheerfully exerting the last
atom of physical strength in teaching a child the letters of
the alphabet. In a like spirit, our evangelist could joyfully
descend from preaching to thousands to the humble occupation of selling a cheap copy of the Scriptures to the
rudest and most illiterate boor that ever attended a Lancashire fair.

If he had little to say regarding himself or his work,
he had a ready tongue for his Master. To prefer Christian
work to Christ Himself, is full of peril to the soul. This is

to make a Christ of work for Him, and to make of Christ a stepping-stone to self. Not so did our evangelist. He sought to keep his heart ever warm in love to his Saviour. "Oh, I wish I could die for Jesus!" he one day said to a friend. In his thrice-repeated question to Peter, "Simon, son of Jonas, lovest thou Me?" our Lord did surely teach His servant that the first and chief qualification for feeding the lambs and the sheep is love to Himself. Intellect, learning, eloquence, are gifts that may be coveted; but the more excellent way is love. He who most loves his Lord is nearest the source of light and power; he is the fittest instrument for the Master to employ. May we not find here the explanation of the marvellous usefulness with which God was pleased to honour Henry Moorhouse?

He was also characterized by a certain transparency and child-likeness. A gracious simplicity is holy greatness. This opens the door and wins a way for the servant of Christ when more brilliant qualities fail. It disarms criticism, breaks down prejudice, and removes offence. "A little child shall lead them." One will receive the bleating lamb, when he spurns the snappish dog. From the man whose character is "one-fold," one feels he has nothing to fear. A natural openness of character, when sanctified by grace, is like the heavens for clearness. After meeting with the commonplace character that is close, knowing, and of too many folds to admit of any full glimpse of the interior —and one meets men of this type every day, both in church and market—it is refreshing and elevating to come upon the single-minded, out-and-out-honest, child-like soul that suspects no evil and inspires no fear, and resembles the well-cut diamond that reflects light at every point, rather than the richly-adorned casket which contains something, you know not what, or may contain nothing at all.

From the gentleness and sweetness of his disposition he

naturally, and without affectation, conducted himself as a
true Christian gentleman. He was the same man, indeed,
in the drawing-room and in the kitchen ; and yet with a
wise difference. I have known an evangelist at the dinner-
table catechise his host and the entire company one by one,
demanding of each a categorical answer to the question,
"Are you born again?" The intention, doubtless, was
good; but so far as the adaptation of means to the end is
concerned, he would have been as near the mark, had he
stuck his fork into his neighbour's ribs, with the view of
improving his digestion. Henry Moorhouse could be very
bold and even blunt, but he did not blunder and spoil his
work in that way. "Are you a Christian?" he inquired of
a gentleman in America, to whom he had just delivered a
letter of introduction. The answer to this question was a
hearty invitation to the supper table and all the hospitalities of the house. But he assured the kind host that his
Master had laid this duty upon his heart, and he dared not
enter upon the enjoyment of any hospitalities until the
question was answered. This persistency of love, for such
it was, served to break the fetter that for a long season had
bound the tongue of his host on the subject of personal
religion, and prepared him for a fresh baptism of grace.
But such things can only be done by men full of the Holy
Ghost and of faith.

"Faithfulness, devotedness, unselfishness, love to the
Master," are the characteristics ascribed to him by his
most intimate friend, Mr. George C. Needham, of Chicago.
A consecrated man, he seemed ever to breathe the free,
loving, joyful spirit of one who has lost his own will in God's.
If he had a place near his Lord, the only station he coveted,
it was the very place occupied of old by the woman who sat
behind Jesus, washing His feet with her tears, and wiping
them with the hair of her head. The remembrance of his

early life never ceased to give him unutterable sorrow. He
could not forgive himself. He who is forgiven by God
never forgives himself. He who forgives himself has never
been forgiven by God. While, in his later years at least,
he entertained an habitual repugnance to any allusion on
his own part to the days of his shame, he cherished the constant recollection of it, and like the sweet singer of Israel,
he had his seasons and psalms, "to bring to remembrance."
A sense of his infinite obligations to his Redeemer was the
predominating emotion of his soul. This lay at the root of
his character and work. Truly he could say—

> " Body, soul, and spirit,
>   O Lord, I give to Thee ;
> A consecrated offering,
>   Thine evermore to be."

Twenty years of life "after the flesh," were never
followed by twenty brighter years "in the Spirit," than the
career of this child-like man reveals.

Moorhouse walked closely with his God. Much prayer
gave him that quietness and confidence in which so largely
lay his strength. It was the wise resolution of the sagacious
American revivalist Nettleton, who was instrumental in the
conversion of many thousands of sinners to Christ, "to
aim at the greatest amount of good with the least possible
noise." This can be accomplished only by a constant
dwelling in the secret place of the Most High. So much
was Moorhouse in the habit of prayer, that he ceased not to
commune with His Lord even in sleep. This may explain
his singular dreams, of which one instance may be here
given. Once in a dream he thought he saw the evangelists
of the day brought into a room for examination. Each was
placed, like a statue, on a pedestal, with a looking-glass on
his naked breast, revealing his besetting sin. A little boy,

like an angel, went round, naming each in turn, and announcing to each his sin. To one, love of money; to
another, praise of men ; to a third, self-exaltation; and so
on. Henry trembled as the little angel-interpreter ap-
proached and intimated to him that his besetting sin was
the love of the praise of men. Of all present, only three
were exempt from every motive save love to Christ. This
was only a dream ; but to the end of his days Henry Moorhouse seemed to live in constant watchfulness against the
snare of human praise.

So much with his Saviour, no wonder if he grew like
Him. His face shone; but he wist not that it shone. He
walked so constantly in the Lord's garden that his garments
were always redolent with its perfume. He carried the
Rose of Sharon in his bosom, and the fragrance was diffused
around. He looked for answers to prayer every day, and he
got answers every day. He prayed about everything, and
he was answered about everything. He was wont to pray
for light on a difficult passage of Scripture, and the light was
given. He prayed for clothes when reduced to a last
and thread-bare suit, and the answer came in the very
things he needed. He prayed for money, when his last
shilling was gone, and the money was sent him. He
prayed for conversions, and conversions followed. When
he had no pressing necessity, he prayed for the love
he had to his God. And when his prayers were not
answered, or were answered " by terrible things in righteousness," he learned therewith to be content. But in his
communion he ever took the Book with him. He seemed
to catch its very whisper, as well as its louder voices. He
walked with God not less by the Word than by prayer. He
laid the Book at the Master's feet and read it there : this
was the spring of his personal holiness, and his evangelistic
power. The Bible was indeed the mirror in which he

beheld the glory of the Lord, and steadfastly looking, he was changed into the same image from glory to glory even as by the Spirit of the Lord. It was the Holy Spirit thus dwelling in him that made Henry Moorhouse a lowly, full-souled, happy disciple, a trusty, single-eyed messenger of the truth, whose silver-voiced trumpet has been the medium of conveying the distinct call of God's effectual grace to many immortal souls.

From hollows and knotty parts the smoothest and most perfectly rounded human character is never wholly exempt; and it were no hard task to discover infirmities and defects in Henry Moorhouse. But taking him altogether, his life as a Christian was singularly free of blame, and his course honourable in a high degree. As a monument of divine grace he was truly remarkable; as a preacher of Christ he was chief of a thousand. In his life's story we see how God stains the pride of man, both in the men He saves, and in the men He employs to save others. No man, with more truth than he, might appropriate the words of the apostle and say, "By the grace of God I am what I am." No evangelist, no pastor, no worker for Christ in these days, has been in his service a better illustration than Henry Moorhouse of the inspired words, "For God hath chosen the foolish things of the world to confound the wise; and God hath chosen the weak things of the world to confound the things which are mighty; and base things of the world, and things which are despised hath God chosen, yea, and things which are not, to bring to nought things that are, that no flesh should glory in His presence."

THE END.